# Tanny McGregor

# ink & Ideas

## SKETCHNOTES for Engagement, comprehension, and Thinking

**HEINEMANN**
Portsmouth, NH

# FAQs!

**Aren't sketchnotes just cute notes, with more decoration than content?**

There's more than meets the eye when it comes to sketchnotes. Discover the why behind this approach to notetaking in Chapter 1, "More Than Just a Pretty Page."

**Isn't sketchnoting just for artsy types?**

You'll be surprised to read about all kinds of brilliant thinkers, past and present, who sketchnote! See the book's opening, "Inking as Thinking."

**How can I teach sketchnoting to my students if I've never tried it myself?**

Not to worry! You can learn along with your students. Find a step-by-step launching lesson in Chapter 2, "One Blank Page = Unlimited Possibilities."

**When sketchnoting, where should I start on the page? How do I know what colors to use?**

With practice, these decisions will come naturally. It might be helpful at first, however, to use Chapter 3, "Becoming an Independent Inker," as your beginner's guide.

**How can I incorporate sketchnoting into what I already do in the classroom?**

There are many ways to merge this practice into your daily literacy and content-area classes. Check out Chapter 4, "Sketchnote LIVE," for dozens of lesson ideas.

Some of my students have difficulty making their thinking visible. Can sketchnoting help?

We can teach kids to organize their thinking with sketchnotes to make it visible and shareable. In Chapter 5, "Thinking Ahead & Thinking After," you'll discover how simple this can be.

My students already sketchnote with text passages. How can we expand the use of this powerful tool beyond the basics?

Once you get started using sketchnotes in unconventional ways, the sky is the limit! A collection of interesting sketchnote applications is located in Chapter 6, "Sketchnote Tapas."

I want to learn more about sketchnotes. Where should I turn?

Reading this book is a good start! There are many other resources available to expand your knowledge and build your repertoire of ideas. "A Sketchnoter's Treasure Trove" can be found in Appendix A.

What's more important in a sketchnote: the thinking or the art?

What if we consider the power of both? Perhaps it's an AND, not an OR. Reading the closing, "Thinkers & Artists," might help you decide.

Starting with a blank page scares me. I think my students might feel the same way. Should we begin with a sketchnoting template?

Glad you asked! The collection of templates in Appendix B will get you started, and soon you'll be creating your own.

**Heinemann**

361 Hanover Street

Portsmouth, NH 03801–3912

www.heinemann.com

*Offices and agents throughout the world*

The author and publisher wish to thank those who have generously given permission to reprint borrowed material:

Figure UN1.04 "Our anchor chart for real reading" from *Comprehension Connections: Bridges to Strategic Reading* by Tanny McGregor. Copyright © 2007 by Tanny McGregor. Published by Heinemann, Portsmouth, NH. Reprinted by permission of the Publisher. All rights reserved.

**Library of Congress Cataloging-in-Publication Data**

Names: McGregor, Tanny, author.
Title: *Ink & ideas : sketchnotes for engagement, comprehension, and thinking* / Tanny McGregor.
Other titles: *Ink and ideas*
Description: Portsmouth, NH : Heinemann, 2018. | Includes bibliographical references.
Identifiers: LCCN 2018018861 | ISBN 9780325092539
Subjects: LCSH: Sketchnoting.
Classification: LCC LB2395.25 .M34 2018 | DDC 371.30281—dc23
LC record available at https://lccn.loc.gov/2018018861

*Editor:* Tobey Antao
*Production Editor:* Sonja S. Chapman
*Cover and interior designs:* Suzanne Heiser
*Typesetter:* Suzanne Heiser
*Illustrations and sketchnotes:* Tanny McGregor
*Manufacturing:* Steve Bernier

Printed in the United States of America on acid-free paper

22  21  20  19  18  VP  1  2  3  4  5

To Dad & Mom

It took thousands of
crayons to raise me,
and your love
taught me to live
outside the lines.

# Contents

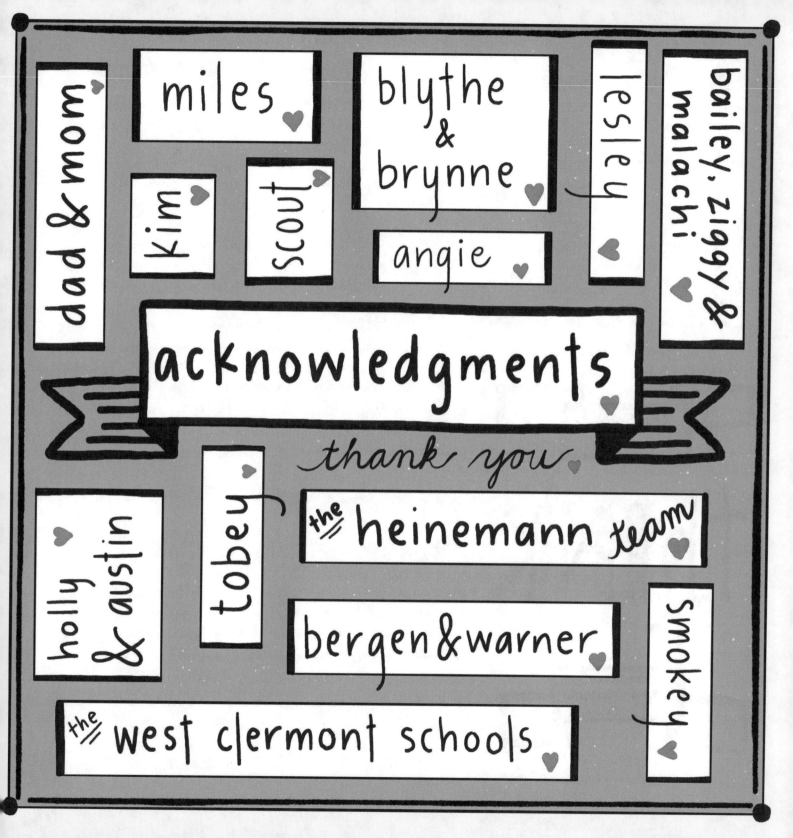

# Inking as Thinking

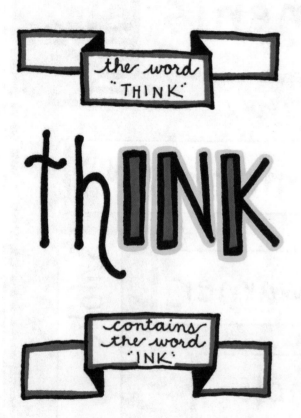

the word "THINK"

thINK

contains the word "INK"

As soon as this book reaches readers, I'm sure to be asked, "So how long did it take you to write it?" Fifty years is the answer I'll give, only because it's true. I've been doodling and sketchnoting since the beginning of my life, and an inky path has led me here. In coming to know my journey, perhaps you'll see a bit of yours, and even if similarities aren't apparent, you're likely to see the faces of your students who want—even need—to doodle and sketch their way to brilliance as you guide their learning.

Thinking with pen in hand runs in my family, just like having blue eyes and freckles. I inherited all of these. Let me tell you about two blue-eyed, freckled relatives of mine: my grandfather and my mother, a sort of sketchnoting through the generations, if you will.

My grandfather Hollis had barely finished elementary school when the tobacco fields called him away. The year was 1910. My grandpa did not have a depth of literacy knowledge behind him as he entered the world of work, but he had a lot of reading to do: the newspaper to keep up with local and world events, the Bible to prepare for Sunday school lessons, letters and ledgers and all that came along with raising a family of twelve and running a 700-acre farm. How did Grandpa read and comprehend all of these things with such a limited education? One thing he did was annotate. Everything. Every time he read. Blue ink surrounded the text, margins full of jots and symbols. And the text itself was under-lined and circled, with arrows jutting out every which way.

My mother, Linda, Hollis' youngest daughter, reads in much the same way, though her formal education is more complete. Receive a birthday card in the mail from my mom? I'll betcha it is annotated, Hallmark's text emphasized, edited, and added to until it is just right. My mother gives away her annotated books, the most personal gift she could give: her own thinking, visually recorded forever.

So I come by this passion for keeping a handwritten record of my thinking in the most natural of ways. I saw those I love think with their brains and their hands at the very same time.

**This photograph of my grandparents was taken in the early 1940s in Somerset, Kentucky. They pose here with the youngest five of their ten children.**

I noticed as a small child, struggling to stay quiet in church, that having a pencil in my hand, doodling away, seemed to comfort me. Calm me down. Help me think about something that was being said.

I noticed that sometimes in school I just wanted to sketch or doodle while I was reading . . . or while the teacher was talking. I noticed that sometimes I was allowed to do this, and some-times it was forbidden.

Around fifth grade I started talking to my friends on the telephone. I noticed that to pay attention to the conversation I tended to jot down words or simply doodle repeated shapes.

As a junior high student I realized that when I studied at home I always had a pen in my hand. Sometimes I sketched images that connected with the content I was studying. Sometimes there was no apparent connection at all.

In high school and college I processed information and merged my own thinking with the text through what Harvard calls *marginalia*. A blank space was an invitation to slow down and think, try out a mnemonic device, draw a symbol or quick sketch.

DAVID ULIN

"I've grown so used to reading with a pen in my hand that I MISS IT with an almost PHYSICAL ACHE when I read for pleasure, AS IF IN THE ACT of ANNOTATION I can't help but take a DEEPER DIVE."

{from "THE LOST ART of READING Why Books Matter—In a Distracted Time"}

And now, when I'm reading or listening, with a book on an airplane or a handout at a conference, I understand with a pen or stylus in my hand. A notebook and a Flair pen. A sketching app and my favorite stylus. Dry-erase markers on a whiteboard. Somehow, someway, please let me sketch! I've read that young Abe Lincoln sketched on a fire shovel when paper and pencil weren't available. I can relate.

Even though I've been exploring doodling and sketchnoting for fifty years, only in the past twenty or so have I been metacognitive about it, *metacog-doodling,* as Lucas, a clever fourth grader, put it. I think about my thinking as I transform a page or screen into a nonlinguistic representation of my thinking. I entered this esteemed sketchnoting society because others showed me how my thoughts might become deeper with a bit of ink and a willingness to slow down and think. This book exists because I believe we can do the same for our students. They are amazing, brilliant humans who deserve every available option for making their thinking known in this world.

## The Sketchnote Society

I've been holding the mirror closely, as my friend Angie says. I'll step back now, moving from personal reflections to historical and contemporary connections. We'll gaze back over our shoulders, to recognize notetakers from the past and look at contemporaries who use this medium to wow the world with their visual thinking. The society of sketchnoters is far-reaching, across time and discipline. All kinds of people sketchnote, for all kinds of reasons.

Consider the following thinkers. If so many genius minds use sketchnoting to think, remember, and create, why wouldn't we offer up this option when thinking across the school day? As you'll soon see, doodling and sketching are nothing new, but to consider practical applications for our students and ourselves is contemporary and exciting!

- **Jean-Michel Basquiat:** *Visual Artist (1962–1988).* Basquiat filled hundreds of pages with his musings, images, poetry, and wordplay. Many of these initial renderings were the foundations of his signature style. Like most of us, he had no formal training. There's even a major traveling exhibition titled "The Unknown Notebooks" that features his creative thinking. Check out #basquiatnotebooks.

- **Alexander Graham Bell:** *Scientist & Inventor (1847–1922).* Bell recorded many of his ideas and experiments in notebooks, which are now preserved by the Library of Congress. His handwriting is scratchy; his sketches are quirky. *The Atlantic* even calls his notebooks "delightfully weird"!

- **William Blake:** *Poet & Painter (1757–1827).* Blake's famous notebook holds sketches, poems, and prose, most in pencil, some in ink. He filled "The Notebook" with densely packed notes, and when he reached the end he turned it upside down and started again.

- **Leonardo da Vinci:** *Painter, Sculptor, Architect, & Engineer (1452–1519).* Da Vinci worked on scraps of paper instead of in a bound book. He is believed to have carried bundles of notes everywhere he went to record observations and explore his curiosities. The collection of his notes is known as The Codex Arundel and contains his famous "mirror writing," written with his left hand and moving right to left.

- **Thomas Alva Edison:** *Inventor & Businessman (1847–1931).* Edison compiled more than five million pages of notes! The Thomas A. Edison Papers Project at Rutgers University archives and analyzes these notebooks, which include everything from research details to reading logs and to-do lists. His notebooks show how he valued the birth of new ideas: they record conceptual inventions and early processes.

- **Albert Einstein:** *Physicist (1879–1955).* The notebooks of Einstein contain the $E=mc^2$ formula in his own handwriting, along with letters to his mother. He developed his theories through sketches, notes, and diagrams. Like so many visual thinkers, Einstein showed his thinking in more than one way. These pages can be viewed at alberteinstein.info.

- **Bill Gates:** *Entrepreneur (1955–).* Gates is known for being an entrepreneur, philanthropist, and investor, but that's not all. Bill Gates is a doodler. He left some of his meeting doodles near the seat of Prime Minister Tony Blair, and it took a while to discover that they actually belonged to Bill. Interesting fact: Gates purchased da Vinci's Codex Leicester in 1994 for over $30 million.

- **Jane Goodall:** *Primatologist (1934–).* For fifty years, Goodall meticulously recorded chimpanzee behavior in hundreds of notebooks that are now archived at Duke University. Often with sketches in the margins, Goodall's notes included color-coded charts of her own design. She created a personalized, visual way to make information meaningful.

- **Jim Henson:** *Puppeteer & Artist (1936–1990).* What couldn't Henson do? Henson sketched, doodled, and storyboarded his way to international fame. Miss Piggy and Kermit started out as a quick sketch!

- **Herbert Hoover:** *Thirty-First President of the United States (1874–1964).* Most U.S. presidents have been doodlers. Hoover was known in his time as a talented doodler, with his sketches purchased for large sums of money and even duplicated as fabric designs.

- **Frida Kahlo:** *Painter (1907–1954).* Ten years' worth of Kahlo's letters, watercolors, sketches, and brightly inked journal entries were kept in a diary, locked away for a time but now published. The pages are filled from edge to edge with intense color and emotion. When viewing her sketchbook, it's as if the pages speak with her strong, questioning voice, in an attempt to make sense of her world.

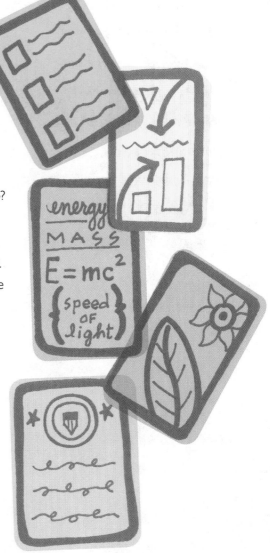

Want to know more about the notebooking explorations of everyday teachers and authors? Visit Amy Ludwig VanDerwater's blog, *Sharing Our Notebooks*. My post, "Notebooks Make Life More Meaningful," was featured on December 10, 2015.

www.sharingournotebooks
.amylv.com/2015/12
/tanny-mcgregor
-notebooks-make
-life-more.html

**John F. Kennedy:** *Thirty-Fifth President of the United States (1917–1963).* Kennedy's sketches and doodles are heavily text-based. Kennedy repeated important words or themes and boxed them in with dividing lines. One archived Kennedy doodle was sketched the night before he was assassinated, or so it is believed.

**Mark Mothersbaugh:** *Composer & Inventor (1950–).* Since the 1970s, Mothersbaugh has been creating one postcard-sized sketch each day. His sketch cards exceed 30,000 now, merging shapes, colors, and text that remind us of the power of the handmade, even when technological advances seem to quickly grab our attention.

**Pablo Picasso:** *Painter & Sculptor (1881–1973).* At times, Picasso made hundreds of conceptual sketches before beginning to paint. He was known for carrying a pocket-sized notebook with him everywhere, and if a pen wasn't available he'd use a pencil stub. He seamlessly combined text and images on page after page.

**Horace Pippin:** *Painter (1888–1946).* Like many mentioned here, Pippin was self-taught. He sketched with a piece of charcoal when he was a kid, and made drawings and paintings for other people as gifts. Nothing could stop him from writing and sketching: not a World War, not paralysis in his arm. He even drew with the iron fire poker in his house. His drawings and paintings were often accompanied by his cursive text on the same page.

**Beatrix Potter:** *Author & Conservationist (1866–1943).* Potter's sketchbooks mixed drawings and paintings with letters written to the children of her friends. She was insatiably curious, and her notes often explored her scientific observations of the natural world.

**Mark Twain:** *Writer & Humorist (1835–1910).* Twain designed his own notebooks and had them custom made, along with self-pasting scrapbooks to make collecting artifacts easier. Many of Twain's note pages are equal parts text and sketch, with a dose of humor thrown in for good measure.

● **Virginia Woolf:** *Writer (1882–1941).* Woolf added to her notebooks on an almost daily basis from 1915 until her death. At times she teamed with her sister, Vanessa Bell, to merge prose and pictures. She noted how adding entries to her notebooks lessened her depression and wondered why she didn't use writing for this purpose more often.

Artists. Writers. Inventors. Scientists. Are you as amazed as I am by these thinkers? And all of them have something in common: visible, visual thinking, created in notebooks, journals, and diaries and on postcards and paper scraps. Words. Pictures. Symbols. Color. Font. Intentional design decisions. When we learn about the visual notetaking habits of great thinkers such as these, it becomes difficult to believe that sketchnoting is not taught and valued in every classroom. When we sketchnote, our thinking has a permanence that it might not otherwise have. When we sketchnote, we discover our own brilliance that might otherwise remain hidden. A different kind of thinking happens with pen in hand.

WORDS and PICTURES

CAN WORK together

TO COMMUNICATE

MORE POWERFULLY

THAN → EITHER → ALONE.

WILLIAM ALBERT ALLARD

## CHAPTER 1

# More Than Just a Pretty Page

## Sketchnoting: Words and Pictures Together

A couple of years ago I went to a local independent theater to see a film recommended by a friend. *Words and Pictures* (2013), starring Clive Owen and Juliette Binoche, ran only a few weeks in my town, but I'm still thinking about one of the threads that ties the plot together. Clive's character, an English teacher, believes in the power of words. Juliette's character, an art instructor, knows how influential pictures can be. Which is stronger: words or pictures? As you can likely infer, the students and teachers reached the same conclusion by the end of the film. Words and pictures together: the true power to communicate lies therein. It's as *National Geographic* photographer William Allard said, "Words and pictures can work together to communicate more powerfully than either alone." Like many of us who have chosen a career in the classroom, I have the teaching gene (if there isn't one, they just haven't discovered it yet) so nearly every movie I see and book I read has some implication for teaching when I stop to think about it. As I sat in the theater with the credits rolling by, I thought about what I knew about thinking made visible, drawn from a career's worth of professional books and workshops. I thought about sketchnoting.

## Sketchnoting is words and pictures together.

Its use is gaining in momentum and credibility in business and education. Like so many popular concepts, though, the topical lexicon can be confusing. At times multiple labels for the same ideas appear in the media and professional literature,

and we often toss words around with meanings that overlap. In other sources, you might read about edusketching, visual notetaking, graphic representation, and a variety of other terms. And then, of course, there is doodling. While this book's focus is on the sketchnote, the doodle is a close relative.

In this book we'll focus on sketchnoting defined as creative, individualized notetaking that uses a mix of linguistic and nonlinguistic representation, aka words and pictures together. Consider sketchnoter Mike Rohde's definition as well: "Sketchnotes are rich visual notes created from a mix of handwriting, drawings, hand-drawn typography, shapes, and visual elements like arrows, boxes, and lines" (2013, 2). It would be a mistake to stop here, though. My colleague Beth Rimer from the Ohio Writing Project takes us where we need to go when she says:

> When I look back at my sketchnotes, I see arrows, bullets, doodles, and lines. My notes look fun, but what I really see with each change in font or with each new sketch are the connections I made, the ideas I remember, and the active learning I did. When I sketchnote or when I teach others how, it's a way to both focus and relax—being active in the learning.

Beth's words are the perfect pathway into this chapter.

## Why Sketchnotes?

We see examples of sketchnotes all around us, as advertisements, in articles, and on social media. We might even be encouraged by colleagues or instructional coaches to include sketchnoting as a response option for our students. Sure, sketchnoting can add some fun and variety to the otherwise routine practice of notetaking, but let's delve deeper into the why and not just be enamored with the how.

- Does sketchnoting align with our beliefs about best practice?
- What benefits do sketchnotes provide for the thinker/reader/writer/listener/viewer?
- What does research suggest about the practice of sketchnoting?
- How important is notetaking, and how does sketchnoting fit in?

As with any instructional strategy, when we read widely and understand deeply, we can move forward with confidence in our teaching. Let's investigate!

## Sketchnotes Are Thinking Made Visible

Perhaps there is no one more influential with regard to the importance of visible thinking than Harvard professor David Perkins, whose brilliant words have been shared, tweeted, and quoted repeatedly, and rightly so. "Imagine learning to dance when the dancers around you are all invisible. Imagine learning a sport when the players who already know the game can't be seen. Bizarre as this may sound, something close to it happens all the time in one very important area of learning: learning to think. Thinking is pretty much invisible. To be sure, sometimes people explain the thoughts behind a particular conclusion, but often they do not. Mostly thinking happens under the hood, with the marvelous engine of our mindbrain" (2003). Invisible thinking stays hidden. Sketchnoting, on the other hand, unleashes a reader's thinking in short order, with colors, shapes, and letters gushing forth to flood the page.

In *Strategies That Work,* Stephanie Harvey and Anne Goudvis (2007) acquaint us with "tracks in the snow" and forever change the way we see the white space on the page. The following passage is covered in pink highlighting tape in my copy of the book: "In the same way that animals leave tracks of their presence, we want readers to 'leave tracks of their thinking.' It is impossible to know what readers are thinking when they read unless they tell us through conversation or written response" (28). Harvey and Goudvis encourage readers to mark and code the text in margins, on sticky notes, and in their notebooks and journals. Sketchnotes can turn up in all of these places and more, as we'll soon see.

No white space is safe when a sketchnoter finds a pen and gets to work. Thinking begins to appear, much like invisible ink under an ultraviolet light. Sketchnoting says to us, "Someone spent time thinking here."

## Sketchnotes Welcome Linguistic and Nonlinguistic Representation

*"I don't have to do it just one way. If it makes sense to use words, I use words. If a picture says it better, then that's what I choose. There are different ways to say the same thing."*

**—Ferguson, college student**

Ferguson is right. And there is science to back her up.

The dual coding theory, proposed by Paivio (1971), attempted to explain how powerful images can be in our thinking. Over the past few decades, the theory has been discussed, debated, and extended. Dual coding bridges images and words, proposing that the verbal code (language) and the nonverbal code (objects and pictures) work together flexibly. At times the verbal code takes precedence, and at other times, the nonverbal code rules our thinking. Words evoke images; images evoke words. Each is stored independently in our brains, though they are linked. Dual coding theory posits that we maximize the chances for recall when words and pictures are stored in two ways in the brain. This multimodal theory has been widely applied to literacy, including comprehension. Sketchnoting takes the dual coding theory and lets it trickle down into the margins of text and into our notebooks, making it practical for our everyday reading and listening.

Not only are images coded differently from words in our brains, but nonlinguistic representation also boosts student achievement with the use of sketches, graphic organizers, and pictographs. In his article, "The Art and Science of Teaching: Representing Knowledge Nonlinguistically," Robert Marzano states, "Nonlinguistic strategies require students to generate a representation of new information that does not rely on language. In the hundreds of action research projects that we have conducted with teachers throughout the years, this approach is one of the most commonly studied. Specifically, across 129 studies in which teachers used nonlinguistic strategies—such as graphic organizers, sketches, and pictographs—with one class but not with another class studying the same content, the average effect was a 17 percentile point gain in student achievement" (2010). These findings don't surprise me. We make meaning in many ways, with words being just one of them. **Sketchnoting opens up the possibilities for response.**

### *Sketchnotes Allow for Student Choice*

With sketchnoting, she who holds the pen holds the power. Only the thinker decides what appears on the page, and how. Zemelman, Daniels, and Hyde call student choice an "indicator of best practice" (2012, 26), and personalized annotation certainly allows for maximum student choice. Our thinking becomes visible because of the choices we make while sketchnoting. A high school English teacher once told me, "I write and sketch to reveal myself to myself." Choice leads to discovery.

Sometimes experienced teachers will connect sketchnotes with mind mapping and concept mapping as "cousins." There are many similarities. Some sketchnotes are, in essence, concept maps. This is important to mention here, because the power of concept mapping rests on student choice. Concept mapping "involves the development of graphical representation of the conceptual structure of the content to be learnt" (Hattie 2009, 168). Hattie found that concept mapping is high-impact and evidence-based. Here's the most important thing about this, as I see it. In his book *Visible Learning*, Hattie states, "The difference between concept mapping and other organizing methods is that it involves the students in the development of the organizational tool" (2009, 168). Visual notetaking is, and should be, all about the student! To have a high impact, Hattie emphasizes that visual representations should summarize main ideas, supporting synthesis and interrelationships. Many sketchnoters, myself included, create concept maps that do all of these things, utilizing color and spatial features to help make comprehension visible and visual.

## *Sketchnotes Help Strengthen the Memory*

A recent study suggests that we remember lectures more fully when we listen and write with pen and paper instead of typing our notes at a keyboard (Mueller and Oppenheimer 2014). The researchers propose that a more shallow kind of processing occurs when notes are typed, because those who type their notes tend to capture lectures word for word. When sketchnoting, it's not about regurgitating passages of text verbatim. It's not about copying or typing from a prepared slide. It's about taking new ideas and information and running them through the brain, mixing and stirring with existing background knowledge to generate new thinking. Sketchnotes help us paraphrase, determine importance, summarize, and synthesize. In turn, we remember.

To extend the ideas from the Mueller and Oppenheimer study, consider what researchers at the University of Waterloo found in 2016 and called the "drawing effect." Wammes, Meade and Fernandes conducted a series of seven experiments to test the benefit of drawing to remember information. The researchers found that drawing enhances memory through an amalgamation of semantic, visual, and motor processing. To add icing to the cake, the researchers found that this drawing effect holds true regardless of how much artistic talent a person has. This means that everyone can benefit from drawings created in visual notetaking. These findings are a cause for celebration. Sketchnoting is an equal-opportunity invitation to deeper thinking while listening, reading, or reflecting. Every classroom can use more response options like that!

Sketchnoting promotes greater recall, "stickier" memories, easier retrieval of information from the brain, and a deeper synthesis of what was read, viewed, or heard. This seems especially important in informational text and in content areas. Author Linda Hoyt has been an ambassador for these ideas for many years.

In my third-grade classroom, Linda's "sketch to stretch" was all of the encouragement I needed to get kids sketching. In her classic title, *Revisit, Reflect, Retell*, Linda describes sketching with text as a "tool for holding onto the content" (2009, 140). She emphasizes thinking as the reason behind the sketching and shows how students use a high level of thinking when stretching their thinking this way. Linda's work gives teachers confidence to take a leap into the unknown world of reading and drawing to deepen comprehension across genres and into the content areas.

### Sketchnotes Make Annotation Thinking-Intensive

We already accept notetaking as a part of classroom life, so let's welcome sketchnotes into the notetaking family! Notetaking as a practice stands the test of time, and for good reason. **Research suggests that taking notes in real time and thinking about those notes later boosts student learning.**

As mentioned earlier, studies tell us that students remember more of what they hear when they write it down. When students take notes, they have higher recall and generate a deeper synthesis than students who don't take notes. It seems the more students record, the better they perform on assessments, especially when metacognitive thought is added to the mix (Bligh 2000; Kiewra et al. 1991; Johnstone and Su 1994). From all accounts, traditional notetaking, when combined with reflection, works. We're not talking about mindless copying here; we're referring to notetaking merged with thinking. From crayons to computers, from notebooks to annotation apps, kids write and record for good reason. We've had research

**TAKING NOTES IS NOT REALLY THE POINT.**

**THE POINT IS TO AVOID reading PASSIVELY.**

Shane PARRISH

to inform us for quite a while now. What can we do to intensify students' thinking while they take notes? Susan Gilroy, a Harvard Librarian at the Lamont and Widener Libraries, advises incoming university students to "make your reading thinking-intensive from start to finish." She likens reading and notetaking to having a dialogue with the author and states that pen or pencil allows for more thinking to be merged with the text . . . a sort of text/thinking cocktail, if you will.

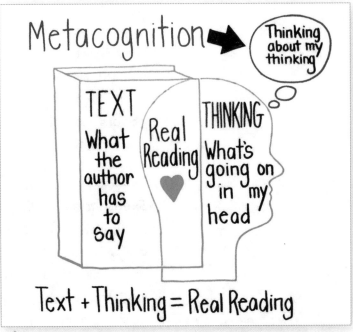

**Chart from *Comprehension Connections: Bridges to Strategic Reading* (McGregor 2007).**

Gilroy's advice is just what students need to hear, but what can teachers do? As part of their work at the Center for Research on Learning and Teaching at the University of Michigan, DeZure, Kaplan, and Deerman suggest that teachers can heighten a student's ability to take meaningful notes by focusing on ways to better engage students. They state that our role as teachers "may require new approaches to time-honored practices" (2001). Enter the sketchnote! As Facebook designer Tanner Christensen says, "To analyze our thoughts—to really understand them or to see what they can become—we have to change what they are" (2018). On his blog, found at creativesomething.net, Christensen recommends writing ideas down to get the most out of them and finding a way to turn them into "something more than simply a mental idea" (2018). Sketchnoting can do this for us. Words and pictures together, a merged map of our thinking with the author's or speaker's ideas. Notetaking turned creative!

When a listener takes notes longhand, he or she is more likely to paraphrase and synthesize information received. This is precisely what we want from the thinkers in our classrooms! There is much more to be studied in this area, though, and the next few years will be interesting ones to watch as the research unfolds. What do we now know for sure? The thinking matters.

### Sketchnotes Enhance Focus and Reduce Stress

Creating artful sketchnotes may do something else for us, something that kids and adults alike desperately need: reduce stress. In a study conducted by Kaimal, Ray, and Muniz (2016), the stress-related hormone cortisol was measured after subjects created visual art. An incredible 75 percent saw a reduction in their cortisol levels. Many people color, doodle, and sketch for this very reason. The best part is that the benefit was not limited to those who consider themselves to be artistic or creative, just as Wammes et al. (2016) found earlier. If we can bring a bit of stress reduction into our classrooms through sketchnoting, let's do it! Our students deserve a relaxed, creative environment in which to flourish, and so do we.

### Sketchnotes Embrace Design

It's the elephant in the room: Are sketchnotes thoughtful design or simply decoration? In spite of all of the research and professional influences, I, like many people, still gravitate toward linguistic communication when I'm responding to text or oral information. I also often offer linguistic response options for my students. Responding with words was emphasized when we were in school, and we carry the linguistic torch, at times neglecting to encourage our students to respond in multiple ways. Sometimes we think about anything other than conventional writing as fluff, as some kind of extra that we'll offer up to kids as a treat or an "if we have time" reward. Year after year, some of our students wish they could show us how thinking drips from the tips of their pens in more ways than one. There's an ingredient missing here that, when added, invigorates our thinking and takes it to levels we didn't know were possible. That ingredient is design.

There are many ways to record thinking that don't rely on the elements of design, and that's all good. Sometimes we just need to quickly capture content or messily scribble down our thoughts before we lose them. These are always options for us, and each serves its purpose. Sketchnoting doesn't sit in opposition to these kinds of notes. In fact, for some students sketching can be the quickest

# Sketchnotes

[More than just a → PRETTY] PAGE

way to make an abstract idea concrete. As we explore sketchnoting processes and products in the pages ahead, let's remember this: Sketchnoting is about thinking *and* design. By merging the two, sketchnotes become both meaningful *and* memorable. Design adds a dimension to our thinking that might seem expendable, but when embraced becomes increasingly valued. Design decisions that involve color, font, and style matter here because they help make our thinking more meaningful. As information designer David McCandless says, "designed information can help us understand the world, cut through BS and reveal the hidden connections, patterns and stories underneath" (www.informationisbeautiful.net).

It's interesting how Target, the department store chain, values design. According to its website, www.corporate.target.com, "It's our belief that great design is fun, energetic, surprising and smart—and it should be accessible and

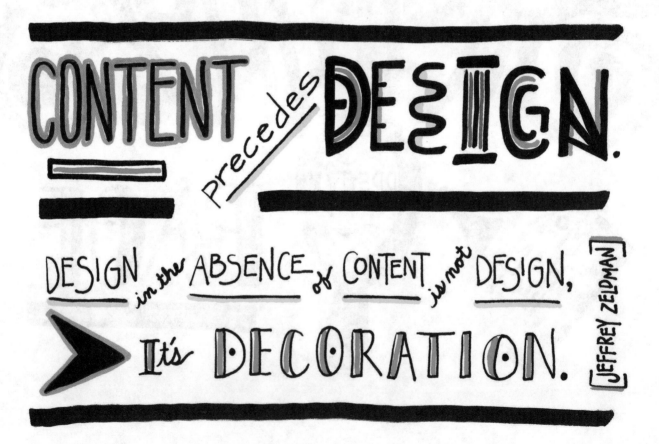

affordable for everyone. When we talk about our dedication to good design, we don't just mean how something looks, but also how it satisfies a need, how it simplifies your life, and how it makes you feel."

In sketchnoting, design plays much the same role. It adds fun, energy, and surprises to our smart thinking and is accessible to anyone, to create or to view. It isn't just about how the sketchnotes look—the design satisfies a need for the simplification of our thinking and links it with emotion. Perhaps researcher Brené Brown (2013) says it best: "Design is a function of connection." We can connect deeply with the content of our learning when design is part of the thinking equation.

We've come a long way since those questions at the beginning of this chapter! So much research to consider, and so many connections to establish. To solidify our thinking as we move into "the what and how" of sketchnoting, we can stand sure on these agreements:

- Sketchnoting is visible thinking that includes words and pictures.
- Sketchnoting honors thinking through offering choice.
- Sketchnoting supports increased memory and focus.
- Sketchnoting promotes deceleration and relaxation.
- Sketchnoting is intentional, designed thinking.

Yes, sketchnotes are way more than just a pretty page. Now get your pens ready. We're about to give it a go.

# A Parent's Perspective on Sketchnoting

**Gwen Barry Blumberg** | PARENT OF A
HIGH SCHOOL STUDENT

My son has always been a doodler. Since he was old enough to hold a pencil, book characters and imaginary creatures have found their way out of the tip of his pencil and onto scraps of paper that all these years later I still find sprinkled throughout various cabinets and drawers in our house.

Since kindergarten, some of his favorite school assignments incorporated and celebrated drawing. In the primary grades, when he was asked to illustrate favorite parts of a story he would divide his paper into shaky panels to show multiple scenes from the text. Asked to show his work in a math problem, he was happy to draw the number of items and then show his thinking with a series of arrows and captions. In fifth grade, he took a keen interest in studying vocabulary because one of the weekly assignments was to illustrate each of his words. Small cartoon characters would cascade down the sides of the workbook pages as he

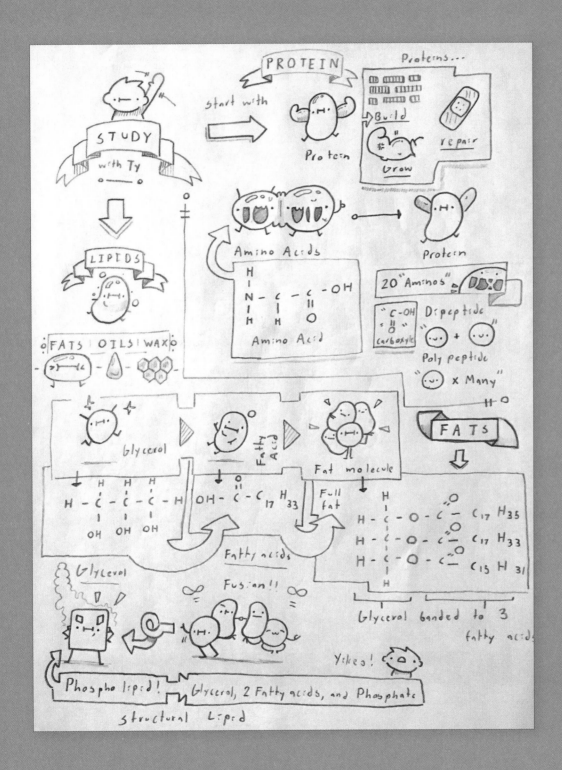

defined words such as *liberate*, *reluctant*, and *evade* with his single-panel sketches. He approached each word with curiosity, gusto, and a well-worn pencil.

As an elementary school teacher and literacy specialist, I have seen the powerful impact of encouraging kids to put pencil to paper in nonstandard ways. I have witnessed firsthand time and time again how a sketch or drawing can help clarify a difficult concept or allow a child to express an idea that might be difficult to put into words. Sketching words and ideas often helps break down the writing inhibitions some children experience when asked to compose in more traditional ways. As a mother, I have always encouraged my son to draw and use illustrations, diagrams, and creative labeling and lettering to organize and clarify his thinking.

Now that my son is in high school, he has merged his love of doodling and his insatiable search for knowledge into a unique style of sketchnoting that is helping him master difficult concepts and deepen his understanding beyond names, places, and dates. In biology, he is drawing amino acids and giving each a unique personality that helps him learn individual characteristics and properties. When the acids combine, he sketches them high-fiving—literally drawing a bond between this abstract concept and the reality of his characters as they come to life on his paper. In Eastern civilization, he is sketchnoting Europe and the Arabian Peninsula and combining doodles, lettering, and invented acronyms to help him internalize new learning. Sketchnoting of this kind requires a synthesis of information beyond rote memorization. It extends information past the short-term memory needed to cram for a quiz.

Sketchnoting gives my son an outlet to his creative interests and enhances his engagement. Because studying with sketchnotes is pleasurable, he spends more time with the material than he would with traditional notes. As a parenting bonus, sketchnoting has become a fun way for my son to share his learning with me; we laugh at the humor in them, and I marvel at his lively and unique approach to his high school subjects.

Long after the textbooks and workbooks of his K–12 career are gone, I have a hunch that his sketchnotes will still be found tucked into the dusty drawers and cabinets of our home. More importantly, the concepts and topics he explored with sketchnotes will remain a part of his collective academic experience and universal understanding.

YOU CAN

## CHAPTER 2

# One Blank Page = Unlimited Possibilities

*So here we are. You, me, and the blank page.*

The sight of a blank page (or screen) might thrill you . . . or terrify you. You might feel excited by the chance to be creative, or you might shut down as the little voice inside your head reminds you that you aren't artistic. Most of us feel some similar combination of emotions every time we embark on a new learning venture or are pulled into new instructional territory. If you love the idea of making sense of your thinking in a visual way, you'll likely devour this chapter without hesitation. If, though, you feel a bit reticent about the vulnerability that sketchnoting seems to bring, and wonder how you could ever feel comfortable trying this in your notebook, much less teach it to your students, this chapter will get you on your way to becoming a fearless sketch-noter. We—and our students—may have what Brené Brown (2015) refers to as "art scars": the creativity injuries we've incurred through the years. Perhaps you can remember a time when a careless comment from a sibling, parent, friend, or teacher reduced your confidence and contributed to a negative self-opinion about your artistic ability. Or maybe you just feel like sketching isn't your strong suit. We're much like our students. Our confidence waxes and wanes with every learning experience. In sketchnoting, your will can triumph over your skill. And the cool thing is, the more you exercise your will, the more opportunities exist for your skill to grow. One brings along the other, if we trust in the process and let our thinking be our guide. A little tolerance for uncertainty will steer you toward success. Don't let page fright get the best of you!

In this chapter, I want to help you get a solid start, both for sketchnoting on your own and for teaching sketchnoting to your students. Here you'll find some sketchnoting basics (a.k.a. tips and tricks), a sample launching lesson to be used with students, ideas for building confidence, and more.

## Square One

 The best part of sketchnoting is, of course, when our thinking bears itself out before our eyes. That's the big picture. It will pay off later, though, if we zoom in to look at the mechanics of sketchnoting now. From choosing a pen to selecting a visual strategy, we'll address it here.

Let's think about materials. What do you need? Ask a dozen sketchnoters about the best pens and paper to use for sketchnoting and you'll likely get a dozen different answers. I think it boils down to three questions. You might not have answers to these questions yet, but as you make sketchnoting a practice your awareness will grow. The same goes for your students!

### 1. What Do You Have Available to You Right Now?

If you have a pencil and a piece of paper, you've got what it takes! I've seen note-takers use everything from crayons to colored pencils to gel pens, and digital sketchnoters use all of those tools in apps, as well. You can plan for other tools to try out later, but don't let the lack of materials keep you from moving forward. It's the same in your classroom, too. Don't try to get it all figured out before you start. Use what you have. You can always embrace new tools, be they analog or digital, as your thinking changes.

### 2. What Do You Enjoy Using?

Think about what tools you like to use. Is there a brand of pens that is your go-to tool? Do you prefer writing with thick or thin lines? And what about paper? Do you like ruled pages, graph paper, or dotted grids? Some of you have instant answers to these questions, and others might never have thought about them before. That's OK. Start with what you like to use and feel comfortable using. Your preferences will follow. As designer Timothy Goodman (2015) says, "Want to change your look? Then change your tool" (11). You'll be surprised at how you'll soon have opinions about what you use and why you use it. Just as the right equipment entices athletes to practice their sports, sketchnoters can become more interested in visual notetaking when preferred tools are accessible. Most of us would choose a pen with a nice ink flow over a broken crayon with a torn wrapper.

That being said, many of us are used to not having a variety of supplies to choose from at school, and making do with the basics is the way many of us operate. We use what we have, of course. But we also realize that a variety of tools might become a priority for us in the future when planning supply orders, making requests from the PTO, or composing our wish lists.

### 3. What Do You Need to Help Show Your Thinking and Make It Meaningful?

It's an interesting dichotomy: Sometimes your thinking comes first, and then it materializes on the page. Other times you don't know what you're thinking until

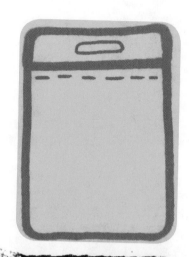

**Materials needed**

Paper (11" x 17" paper can be fun), colored pencils or pens, photographs of sketchnote examples across grade levels, a picture book of your choice, and a way to model your own thinking (chart paper, document camera, whiteboard, etc.)

it exits the pen. Be sure about this: If you are open to exploring your thinking with what you are reading, listening to, or viewing, then you can sketchnote. You'll soon discover if you need a variety of colors to best show your thinking, if you need a quiet workspace, if you prefer working "in the moment" or "after the fact." You'll know what you need as you practice and become more aware of your own thinking and how you want to show it. Exploring sketchnoting in the classroom gives your students the opportunity to learn these things, too. To quote Goodman (2015) again, "Like anything in life, the more you practice and work at something, the better your instincts become" (10). In this way, sketchnoting fosters metacognition. It's a vehicle to help us think about our thinking. The pens, paper, and apps we use aren't the "be all, end all"; they change with us over time as our thinking grows and changes. The "stuff" of sketchnoting contributes to the process. The media helps move the message. Maybe you'll use pens and paper at times, in notebooks and on anchor charts. Your students will, too. Depending on the technology available, you also might sketchnote under a document camera or on an interactive whiteboard with a stylus. When the time comes to change the tools, the metacognitive teacher knows.

For now, let's look at a practical launch for use in the classroom with your students.

## Launching Sketchnoting with Your Students

There are many ways to introduce sketchnoting to kids. The launching experience I'll describe here has been shared with teachers and students across grade levels and content areas, at workshops, in conferences, and in classrooms. Consider sharing the following ideas in one block of time, or segment it over days as time permits. Take it and make it your own. You're the one who makes it meaningful. If you're already a sketchnoter yourself, great. If not, no matter. You'll learn right along with your students in this lesson, and that can even have its benefits, with kids seeing your openness to something new! Don't kids love it when you're learning alongside them? I've always found this to be true.

### *A Heartfelt Beginning and Impressive Research*

I begin with a picture of my grandfather, projected on the screen in the classroom. "His name was Hollis, and he was born in 1900. He didn't have a great education, but he was a great thinker." I share my grandpa's story with the kids, just as I did with you earlier in this book. I want kids to know my "heart" reason for sharing sketchnoting with them: Sketchnoting is more than a reading strategy; it's a way to share my thinking with the world in a meaningful way. What is your "Hollis" story? Do you know a sketchnoter whose notes have piqued your curiosity? Show a picture of them and/or their sketchnotes. Or maybe you saw an example on Twitter or read an article about doodling. Share it. The point here is to share the seed that started growing for you, and where it is leading your thinking. Curiosity is contagious.

"Today we'll try an approach to notetaking that is a little out of the ordinary. For as long as we can tell, people have shown their thinking in visual ways. Through the years, many scientists, inventors, artists, mathematicians, and writers have kept track of their thinking with words and pictures in their notebooks. If all of these brilliant people do this to deepen their thinking, why shouldn't we give it a try in our classroom?" If appropriate, share a few examples of great minds who sketchnoted their way to brilliance. An ideal way to do this is by sharing examples from *Notable Notebooks: Scientists and Their Writings* by Jessica Fries-Gaither (2017). A Columbus, Ohio, science teacher, Jessica shows kids that scientists keep notebooks full of sketches and ideas as a way to record their thinking in meaningful ways. There are plenty of examples here with actual photographs of sketchnotes from scientists and Jessica's Ohio students. It shows how sketchnoting is used beyond the classroom walls, and that all kinds of people use it because they choose to!

Even with primary students, I'll reveal the connection to research. "Did you know that people are studying this kind of special notetaking and are finding some amazing benefits? Researchers find that we remember things longer when we draw them, and our comprehension of tough ideas or text can be deeper if we read or listen while writing and drawing our thinking." If your students are interested and ready for it, share a couple of studies and their findings. I was recently in a third-grade classroom where the students asked me what the researchers found out. Kids need to know the "why" just as we do. Jackie Andrade's study (2010) where the results suggested we remember 29 percent more if we doodle/draw while processing information, is often a great example to mention. I'll tell kids, "None of us can read and remember everything. Researchers are telling us that we can understand and remember more if we do our deep thinking with a pen in our hands and make our thinking visible. It will be fun to explore this together!"

As you might have noticed, this launching experience begins with story and substance, which is a great way to introduce something new. Tell your "Hollis" story to hook the listener and make this lesson memorable, as well as the substantive "why" with connections to research. Now you can get somewhere!

If I haven't already, I will now take time to notice and name this investigation into visual notetaking. "There are many ways to name what we've been talking about. Let's call it 'sketchnoting.' Many designers and writers use this word to describe what I'm about to show you. It's like you are taking notes, but you aren't limited to the written word. You can use whatever you need to represent what's going on in your head: lines, curves, symbols, colors, simple pictures, words, phrases, and more!" I show the term on the screen or write it on chart paper and web the reasons why this is relevant to us. You can, of course, use the graphic I made, but creating one in the moment with your students might be more meaningful.

## A Peek at Others' Sketchnotes

"I think you'll get a better idea of what sketchnotes are if you see some examples that other kids have made. Let's look at a few sketchnotes that were created in different classes at various grade levels." I have gathered actual

**This first-grade student read a couple of books about Abraham Lincoln, then created a timeline-style sketchnote containing interesting events from the texts. Notice Abe at school and Abe on his wedding day!**

sketchnote samples from students and colleagues and have a collection I found on the Web from the notebooks of famous sketchnoters. Perhaps the best way to find samples to share is to look at #readsketchthink on Twitter. There are so many ideas for using sketchnotes there.

**Synthesis of *Seedfolks*.** Ben, grade 5, sketchnoted a quick summary of each chapter in the book with a great balance of words and pictures. This is a simple, effective way to capture a lengthy text over time. *Seedfolks* by Paul Fleischman was read aloud in class, and some students chose to make their thinking visible with sketches.

**Sophia sketches right beside the text, lifting a line here and there, then adding colors and symbols to show the gist of each chunk of information.**

**In response to a poem, high-school student Amor organizes her thinking using frames or containers and fills them with her reactions to the poet's words.**

As we take a look at a variety of examples, I note how young kids, older kids, and adults all use sketchnoting to capture their thinking. We notice that sketchnotes are used in reading, math, social studies, science, art, music—really anywhere. Then I'll ask, "What else do you notice?" Responses typically include:

- Sketchnotes can use color but they don't have to.
- Some sketchnotes contain more pictures than words.
- Some sketchnotes use more words than pictures.
- Everyone sketchnotes in their own way.
- Sketchnoting is not about finding the "right answer."
- You don't have to be a great artist to sketchnote.

## Letting Go of Perfection

As kids begin noticing what sketchnotes can be, and how people of all ages and artistic abilities successfully use visual notetaking to deepen their thinking, it is an ideal time to provide a dose of reassurance: You don't have to be an artist to be a sketchnoter. I want kids and teachers to hear that mistakes are opportunities, and that quick sketches are what we're after, not detailed, realistic pieces of art. I want them to believe they can do this and that it will, indeed, benefit them in

ways they might not anticipate. I want to hit these messages home. How can I do this in a way that invites honesty and thought? There's a picture book for that (or two or three)! I have used a few of them to kindle this conversation with teachers and students. Take a look yourself and see what messages resonate with you. Then choose one or two to read with your students to prepare their hearts and minds for what's next.

To enjoy with your students:

***Beautiful Oops* by Barney Saltzberg** (Workman Publishing, 2010). This book can be fully appreciated only with an actual copy in your hand. Unexpected features on each page surprise the reader, reminding us to let go of unrealistic expectations so something beautiful can happen! While reading this book, I was reminded that creativity is often born from frustration.

***The Girl Who Never Made Mistakes* by Mark Pett and Gary Rubinstein** (Sourcebooks Jabberwocky, 2011). This one's for the perfectionist in all of us. How do you handle it when you make a mistake? You'll feel for the main character as she messes up in a very public way and teaches us how to move on and become a better version of ourselves.

***Walk On! A Guide for Babies of All Ages* by Marla Frazee** (HMH Books for Young Readers, 2006). We're all learning, all the time. Frazee uses the analogy of a baby learning to walk to teach us about falling down, getting up, and why it's worth it to keep on trying.

***Ish* by Peter Reynolds** (Candlewick, 2004). Thanks to this book, many classrooms have adopted the word "ish" as their growth-mindset learning mantra. The way to create something is *your* way. Getting it right is over-rated. Making it meaningful is the aim.

No matter which of these titles you choose (or which great title of your own choosing), pull your students up close and enjoy the book's message while letting students know what sketchnoting is and what it is not. It is visual thinking. It is creative. It is meaningful. It is not perfect. It is not about creating a work of art. It is nothing to be afraid of.

## The Sketchnote Lexicon: Experimenting with a Visual Vocabulary

Just as we accumulate oral and written vocabularies during the course of a lifetime, we can build visual vocabularies, too. Think of it as creating a sketchnoting lexicon. With an introduction to a few foundational features, you and your students will soon be ready to tackle all text types. Really, you will!

**Tip** Want ideas to increase your sketchnote lexicon? Caldecott medal-winning artist and illustrator Ed Emberley can help. Emberley believes everyone can draw, and his books show you how to sketch just about anything you can think of, using simple lines and shapes that everyone can draw. Here's how great *Ed Emberly's Drawing Book: Make a World* is—the first version came out in 1972, and it's still in print.

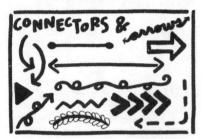

Think about how we build vocabulary: Exposure to words. Playing around with words. Practice using words. Thinking about context for words. More practice with words. From the time we start tinkering around with language we grow in leaps and bounds. We never think that we are "finished" learning language; we learn new words and solidify our understanding of previously learned words with each new conversation and text we encounter. Our oral and written word collections, or lexicons, grow naturally, and it's no different with visual vocabulary. Once you begin to notice the possibilities for an increased visual vocabulary, your awareness opens up a new kind of exposure to the visual barrage around you. You can become a collector of visual vocabulary images with surprising ease.

With students, I might say, "No matter how you feel about yourself as an artist, you can represent your thinking in sketchnotes if you know a few basic features. Let's try them out together!" We move through the features one at a time. I show various examples of each on the screen. Here, and on the following pages, I'll share a collection of options for each feature—both simplified, black-and-white examples to help introduce concepts and colorful reference charts for considering further options. Most all of them are easy to replicate, and there's enough choice here for everyone to get started.

As I show the examples, I sketch a few of my own right there on the spot on sticky chart paper for all to see. As we all try out each new feature, we talk informally about when this feature might help us capture our thinking or represent something we read, heard, or viewed. Oh, and there's music. Don't forget the sketching music! Having a sketchnoting soundtrack is an extra ingredient to make learning the basic features feel special. Plus, I've found that having a musical backdrop can help students relax and enhance their creative flow. For me, listening and sketching unlocks my thinking, and many of my students agree. Favorite artists to listen to while sketchnoting are Vince Guaraldi, The Faux Frenchmen, and Yo-Yo Ma. Instrumentals work best, with no lyrics as distractors.

Here I'll take each sketchnote basic, show examples, and list possibilities my students and I have thought of for when this feature might come in handy.

31

CONNECTORS & ARROWS

ONSHIPS BETWEEN IDEAS, CONCEPTS, CHARACTERS... JUST ANYTHING! CAUSE & EFFECT. CONNECTIONS TO TEXT. SEQUENCES. ANY TIME ONE THING LEADS TO ANOTHER! SHOW RELATI

C·O·N·N·E·C·T·O·R·S & arrows

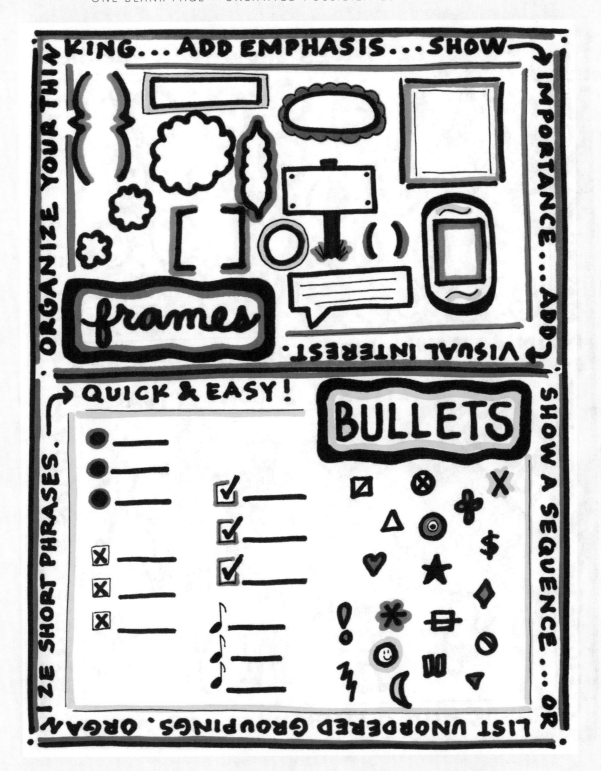

FACES & FIGURES

WORD PICTURES

To help students remember and encourage the use of sketchnote features beyond the launching lesson, New Hampshire teacher Kitri creates anchor charts like this one to keep track of the features for her students. These charts can be referred to and added to over time, with students creating new features to share and post.

Paper and pencil will do for this launching experience, but adding colored pencils and markers will make it more interesting. I often take it a step further by creating a sketchmat to get students started. Created by hand on an 11" x 17" piece of paper, this large area on which to experiment engages students and anchors the experience. Most copy machines reproduce at this size, and many schools stock 11" x 17" paper. Here's an example.

**Sketchmat for a launching lesson (See also Appendix B, page 149)**

After we've tried out these features and had a bit of conversation around them, we take author Austin Kleon's suggestion and "steal like an artist." A gallery walk does the trick. Everyone walks around to admire the work of others, noticing the creativity and individuality on the mats. "If you see something that you didn't think of and would like to add it to your sketchmat, feel free!" Music playing during the gallery walk helps make it feel collaborative.

Quick recap: So far in this launching experience, we've generated curiosity about sketchnoting with a simple story, grounded the practice with research, and with the aid of a picture book, helped to alleviate kids' fears about the vulnerability of creating (and our own fears, too). We have explored the basic features of sketchnoting, practicing in a nonthreatening, music-filled environment, and have talked with students about when these features might be useful and important to us. Now it's time to take a sketchnoting test drive.

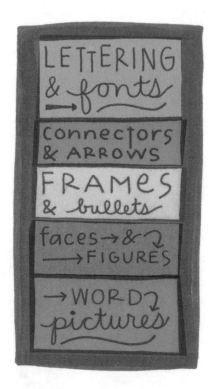

### Try It with Text

Choosing a piece of text for the first whole-group try is interesting. One might think that a good pick would be a simple story or nonfiction piece that most in the class could read and comprehend at some level. You could certainly do that. I've surprised myself, though, by going with a piece of informational text that is densely packed with information: facts, measurements, and descriptions. With sketchnoting as a scaffold, I've seen students take on a piece of otherwise difficult text with pen in hand and meet with success. Sometimes "complex helps you find your simple" when sketching. It can be an exercise in determining importance, in sifting through the text to find the things you *do* understand.

An example of a text that I've used during a launching lesson is an informative piece about the invasive species kudzu. An interesting, unfamiliar topic for many of my students, we sketch and talk our way through a few paragraphs. You can use an excerpt from an article, a page from a textbook, or a chapter from a read-aloud—any text that will give your students a chance to chew on the content and reformulate it with a measure of their thinking added in.

I sketchnote live on chart paper or under the document camera while kids dip in and out of the text. Our cycle is read, think, sketch, repeat. Kids are encouraged to use a combination of words and pictures, constantly asking themselves, "What is most important here?" and "What do I find to be interesting?"

Time is a gift to be given here. That's so easy for me to write, but sometimes difficult to bestow. Be patient as students spend time with the text, and encourage them to sketchnote what they understand. Explain that doing this can loosen up the text that they don't understand, shedding a little light on the tough parts.

However you choose to launch this practice, the experience is not complete without reflection. Be sure to allow for a metacognitive moment. Ask your students one or more of these questions:

- How can sketchnoting help you?
- When might you try it next?
- Can you think of a time when sketchnoting might be useful in math? Science? Social studies? Other classes?

**Here's how a few students (and a teacher!) answered these questions.**

I might use sketchnoteing when I read, am read to, and reading with some one, and silent reading time and now. (n O w) Heart Sketchnoteing

I might use Sketchnoting when I want to think about how the character looks like or when I want to write down fact about the book. Sketchnoting helps me figure out the problem and the solution it helps me think about the seen in my head. I also think it age because It allouse us to imagine what the object might look like. It helps us feel the emochion and there person aletys.

Being older, and always taught to "take notes", sketchnoting does not come easy to me. However, I have always had a creative side, and I love the freedom sketchnoting provides. I can use pictures, symbols, words, figures, etc. to record my thinking.

Will some of your students fall in love with sketchnoting and want to use it whenever they can? No doubt. Will *every* student enjoy sketchnoting and find it useful as a mnemonic and comprehension tool? Unlikely. It's as behavioral sustainability scientist Michelle Segar says in Eric Zimmer's July 2016 interview from *The One You Feed* podcast: "Something is never going to work for everyone, and we always have to keep that in mind whenever we're listening to an author or science or anything." One of the great honors we have as teachers, however, is to add to a student's repertoire of possibilities for problem solving, even for thinking. We teach skills and strategies every day in our classrooms, and sketchnoting is yet another way to think. Recognizing it as a viable option for thinking is what this launching experience is all about.

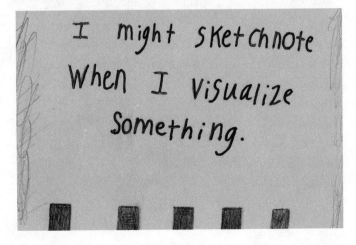

# Learning Alongside Students with Sketchnotes

## Meghan | SEVENTH-GRADE ELA TEACHER

A district professional day was right around the corner, and I had a decision to make. Should I stick with sessions where I'm comfortable? Or should I step out into the unknown? Where would I learn the most? As I selected my workshop sessions on the sign-up doc, I checked the box for "Sketchnoting for Deeper Comprehension." It would be unlikely that I'd ever try an approach to reading response like this on my own, so why not see what this was all about? After all, I did want to add hands-on, student-centered approaches to my classroom. Plus, arts opportunities for my students had been reduced in recent years. My kids deserved more chances to create.

The first time I tried sketchnoting was in the company of colleagues. We learned about supporting research and looked at examples of sketchnotes from across grade levels and content areas. I learned a few easy ways to make notes

Andrew's sketchnote. Andrew: "This is the way I like to learn. I was so happy when we could show our thinking with words and pictures the way we wanted to."

more visual, and by the end of the session had created a basic sketchnote of my own. I could not wait to try this with my seventh graders!

I didn't waste any time. The next week I shared with my students. "Hey, we're going to try something different. I've just been learning about it myself." I shared my first sketchnoting attempt, told the story of my new learning, and shared examples from other middle school students that I found online. I let my students know that I am not an artist, and that my sketchnotes aren't perfect, but they show my thinking.

I tried it with them first. We sketched during a read-aloud. They immediately loved the freedom to express themselves. They loved that their work didn't have to show "the answer" or look like someone else's. I took photos to share with my other classes later in the day.

Some kids found sketchnoting to be hard. They wanted me to show them "the right way." The openness of sketchnoting was scary for them. I told them, "It's OK! It's a new experience for all of us! Just give it a try and see what happens." Some kids wanted to take a quick gallery walk to get ideas from others. When other teachers happened to be in my room they joined in the sketchnoting, too. I'll never forget my last class of the day (for many reasons!) and how they responded to this kind of visual notetaking. These kids needed structure, if you know what I mean. I was afraid to try sketchnoting, but I was shocked at their reaction. They were listening. They were engaged. When they came to class the next day, I heard, "Can we get the markers out?" Their sketchnotes were so interesting I wanted to keep them all. I could see a deeper understanding of the text in their sketchnotes and hear it in their connections and questions. One student, Andrew, seemed to be pulled into the text in ways that I hadn't seen before. Sketchnotes helped him focus and remember what he read.

This year I'll try sketchnoting in new ways, and again I'll be learning along with my students. Our first experience will be with Poe's *The Cask of Amontillado.* Now those will be some interesting sketchnotes!

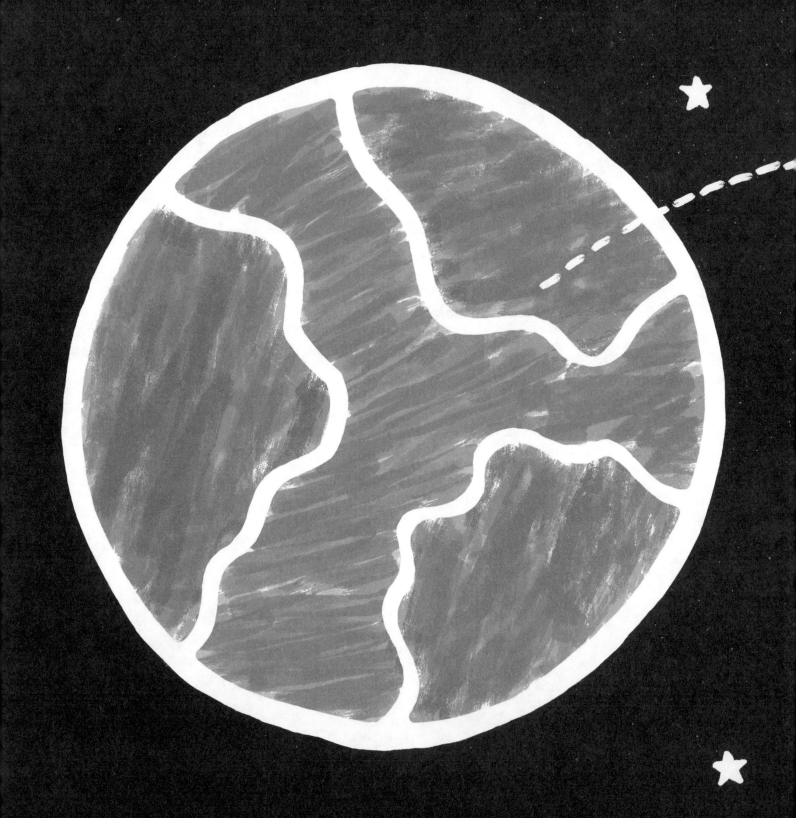

## CHAPTER 3

# Becoming an Independent Inker

When my dear friend Karen and I met in graduate school, we were also holding down full-time jobs and raising families. We were strapped for time, burning the candle at both ends, without much time for ourselves. Reflection wasn't really part of our daily routines; survival was. Our coursework was tough. As we tried to take it day by day, though, we couldn't help but notice how differently we approached each task. I tended to jump right in, without much thought to detail, thinking big picture and leaving the little things until later. Unlike me, Karen was a methodical thinker. A planner. She put way more time in on the front end of a task, hesitating to go too far too fast. There are, of course, pros and cons to the way each of us work. In spite of the dizzying pace at which we were living our lives, Karen and I learned so much about ourselves as we worked together. Because of Karen's differing work style, I began to under-stand my own more fully.

If you are more like me, you might not feel the need for this chapter at this moment. You've read the research and rationale about sketchnoting, so you're ready to jump in the deep end. For you, this chapter might best be saved for later. Come back to it after you've racked up some big-picture experience and are ready for details. If you're more like Karen, however, this is the logical next step in your sketchnoting journey. You might have lingering questions, like *where do I start on the page?* Or *how do I know what to write/sketch first?* This chapter will help you develop some ideas ahead of time, so when you're in the moment you can be ready for some independent inking! And for those of you who decide to hold on to this chapter for later, you'll know when you need it—and you'll likely need it when teaching students how to make decisions in *their* sketchnoting practice. This chapter is written for you as a creator of sketchnotes and as a teacher of sketchnoting. What you learn about yourself makes you better equipped to help kids learn about themselves.

Let's delve into some ideas about spaces, colors, and content: the where, the how, and the what. These can help you and your students express your thinking with colorful clarity.

## Where Shall I Make My Mark?

Children's author and illustrator Melissa Sweet says, "You don't have to know what you're going to create. You just have to begin" (http://melissasweet.net.). I've found this to be true. When sketchnoting in the moment, it is helpful to trust in the process. You won't likely have a mental image of the finished product when the first marks are made. You can have a framework in mind, though, to help the sketchnote to take shape. When I'm sketchnoting, I vary the structure on the page depending on what I think will best allow me to capture what's important and/or interesting from what I'm reading, viewing, or listening to. The more we practice, the better we're able to select an armature and adapt it as necessary during the process. The upcoming five examples are organized from most structured to least. I've purposely created these examples in the most basic way, leaving style to you.

**Tip** Simply rotate the screen or notebook page for a completely different feel. Do you prefer landscape or portrait? Left- or right-handedness might make a difference in your choice, or maybe the amount of table-desk-lap space you have might dictate one page orientation over another.

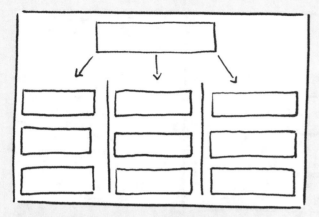

The topic is front and center here, with a double- or triple-entry journal feel underneath. This approach provides high structure and works great for informational content with predictable organization. Still, the sketchnoter makes decisions about what the columns represent and where connecting details belong.

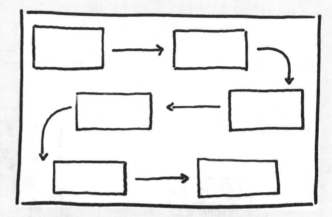

Go with the flow . . . flow chart, that is. Let one thing lead to another, literally. Move vertically, horizontally, diagonally, or a combination of any or all directions.

First-grade teacher Jill modeled her thinking on chart paper as she read an article with her students. Jill's sketchnotes were organized in rows and columns. The title of the article helped Jill decide how to proceed.

Jessica, a science teacher, showed her thinking in a sketchnote as students began to learn new content.

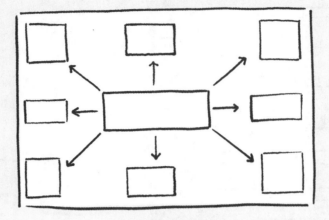

Start in the center with the title or big idea, then let thinking radiate out toward the edges of the space. Add your own style by changing up the containing shapes and the kinds of arrows and connectors. This structure is not confining and allows some flexibility but is still centered and feels planned.

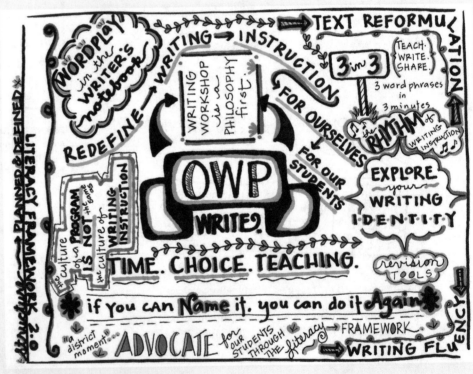

I created this in-the-moment sketchnote during an Ohio Writing Project workshop, starting in the center with the topic. You can see my progress in the three images as I encircled the OWP banner with nuggets of wisdom I learned throughout the day.

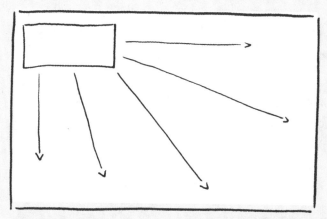

Choose a starting point and sketchnote toward the corners of the screen or page. The starting point shown here is in the upper-left corner, but any corner or other spot will do. Work around the page in a clockwise or counterclockwise motion. There's a lot of freedom in this approach.

The plan here is to not have a plan: Let moment-to-moment decision-making guide you. I have tried all of the approaches listed here, but most frequently I let the structure unfold as the text does. This is the least restrictive approach.

Instructional coach Joy sketchnoted live during a conference session. She began in the upper-left corner and sketched her way out toward the edges of the space.

Taylor, a third-grade sketchnoter, maximized the space on the page with in-the-moment placement decisions as she read. She's a natural when it comes to spatial design!

It's fun to try all of these entry points on the page and see what feels comfortable and meaningful to you. Just knowing the options lets you make a choice that matches what you want to show in the way you want to show it. You might find a favorite and stick with it for a while, or you might constantly ask yourself at the beginning of a sketchnote: From what I know about this topic or text, how might my thinking unfold? Like all things related to learning, a bit of metacognition will serve you well.

## Color Considerations

We make color choices so frequently across the day that we may not realize it. Getting dressed each morning at home. Creating a hallway display at school. Selecting products from the shelf at the market. We have opinions about color, and we're influenced by it, knowingly and unknowingly. Just as color is imporant in our everyday lives, it is laced with emotion and is an integral part of great design.

When sketchnoting, color can help us show the importance of a word or concept. It can help us express what the text made us feel, and sometimes the color alone communicates when words fail. Students have told me that part of the fun of the sketchnoting experience is the option to add colors of their own choosing. Engagement often increases with the addition of color-filled tools with which to experiment.

*"Colors make my sketchnotes look the way I want them to. I'm not always happy with plain black-and-white notes."*

**—Thomas, grade 2**

*"Adding color makes my sketchnotes pop out and makes me want to look at them more. When my teacher gives us the choice to add color it makes me happy."*

**—Tallulah, grade 4**

*"The use of color lets me capture how I'm feeling."*

**— Geovanny, college student**

*"The variety that color provides gives me plenty of choices along the way, and it can help me showcase what I want to remember."*
— **Stewart, art teacher**

In my sketchnotes, I think I've violated every rule there is about design and color. As I mentioned earlier, I tend to just put pen to paper and see what happens. Sometimes I'm pleased with the results, but other times I learn what I don't want to do the next time around. Because that approach isn't appealing to everyone, we can become familiar with a few timeless formulas based on a concept called color harmony. Color harmony helps you answer the question: Which colors go together, and which ones don't? Use the following ideas as a guide, but remember: In the end it's up to you. These are *your* sketchnotes, so there is no right or wrong. Sketchnotes are about content *and* design, so you'll begin to have your reasons why you go with a particular color or scheme on the page. With the following ideas, however, at least you can begin to think about color in a new way and make intentional color decisions to imbue your notes with meaning . . . and help your students to do the same.

Remember primary, secondary, and tertiary colors?  You know, blue and yellow make green and all the rest? Maybe you learned about them in elementary school. That's where it all starts. The primary, secondary, and tertiary colors are arranged on the color wheel like this.

**The three primary colors (red, yellow, blue) combine to make secondary colors (orange, green, purple). The possibilities expand when mixing primary and secondary colors to create tertiary colors (vermillion, amber, chartreuse, teal, violet, magenta).**

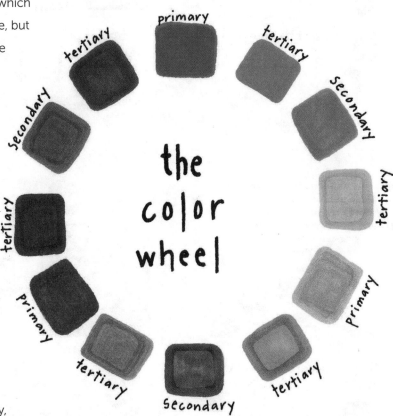

the color wheel

Just like the structured placement choices previously shared to help sketchnoters decide where to first make a mark on the page, here are some basic color schemes to try, straight from the color wheel. Each color scheme option is followed by a digital sketchnote mockup. What do you like? Which will you try?

**Sometimes basic is best. Pick a color, any color, and stick with it throughout the sketchnote. Try pairing black or gray with your color of choice for strong and clear visual notes.**

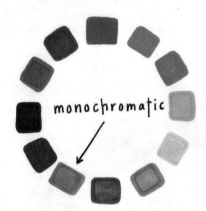

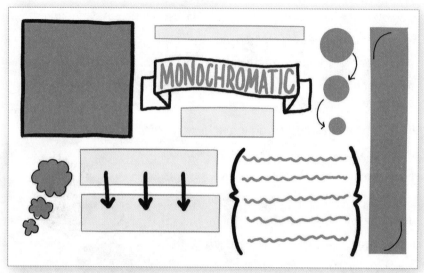

**Monochromatic color scheme**

**Spread out along the color wheel for an analogous color scheme. Just choose a color, then include the colors on either side. This is an easy, never-fail way to create a palette for notetaking.**

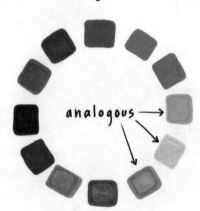

**Analogous color scheme**

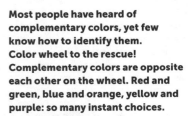

Most people have heard of complementary colors, yet few know how to identify them. Color wheel to the rescue! Complementary colors are opposite each other on the wheel. Red and green, blue and orange, yellow and purple: so many instant choices.

**Complementary color scheme**

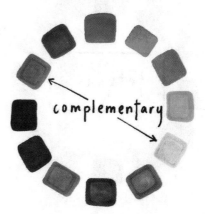

Make an equilateral triangle inside the color wheel, and you'll find three colors that work well together. So many possibilities for visually pleasing combinations.

**Triadic color scheme**

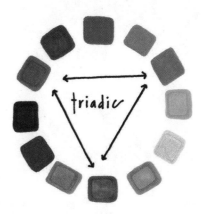

**If you make a rectangle inside the color wheel, you'll find four colors to work with to add detail and interest to your sketchnotes. With four colors, you might use one more heavily throughout, with the other three as accents or to draw attention to specific features.**

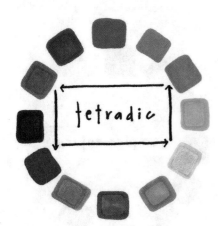

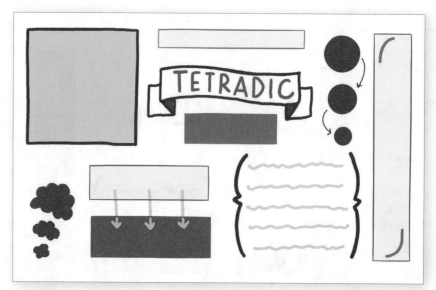

**Tetradic color scheme**

If using pens to sketchnote, experiment with the colors you have. If sketchnoting in an app, there is likely a color-mixing palette at your disposal. If so, you can create any hue or saturation you want. Play around. See what you come up with!

So there are those of us who feel comfortable knowing the "rules" about color and will think about these schemes while sketchnoting. And there are those of us who say, "Rules? What rules? I'll choose the colors I want when I want!" There is a middle ground, though, that might just suit you well. It's called the 60-30-10 rule, and it's a quick, clear-cut way to make color decisions like a pro.

Here's how simple it is. Settle on three colors for your sketchnoting palette. Choose an anchor color, often a dark color or neutral. This color will account for about 60 percent of the sketchnotes you produce on the page. Select an accessory color next, something that partners well with the anchor. This color will be used around half as much as the anchor. For a little fun, have a third color ready as an accent. This color is used sparingly, but makes the 60-30-10 color scheme come together with a designer feel. Save the accent color for important ideas that will leap off of the page when you view. When I first learned about 60-30-10, I began seeing it at work in many everyday places: outfits displayed in clothing stores, IKEA advertisements, and even in the presentation slides from some of my favorite authors. Rules are made to be broken, so don't get hung up on the percentages. Think of 60-30-10 as a framework and let your eyes and your brain make color decisions as you go. In sketchnoting as in life, do what's right for you.

**Here's an antithetical conclusion to a section about color: Sometimes you might not want or need to add color to your sketchnotes at all.** Sometimes a pencil will do, or an ink pen. A black or gray-scale digital sketchnote is sometimes not just what is easiest; it's what is best. There are many times when I'm sketchnoting quickly as I listen to a speaker at a conference, a podcast, or maybe a TED talk. No time for color changes as I'm grabbing every bit of important, interesting content.

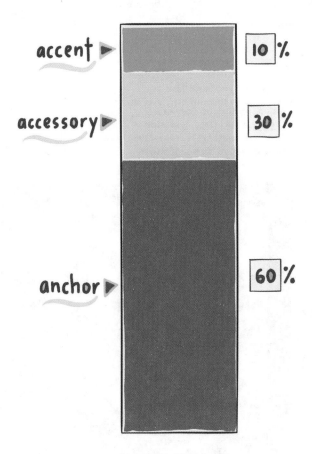

**The 60-30-10 Rule**

55

Other times it's not necessity that dictates a black-and-white graphic representation, it's choice. If I want to show my thinking in a stark portrayal with no detractors, the lack of color can actually emit a message all its own.

Going colorful (or not) is your decision to make. Try not to let all of the possibilities overwhelm you. Instead, think of them as an endless pile of gifts to open.

**A sketchnote summary of a professional learning session at The Cincinnati Art Museum. No time for color. No need, either.**

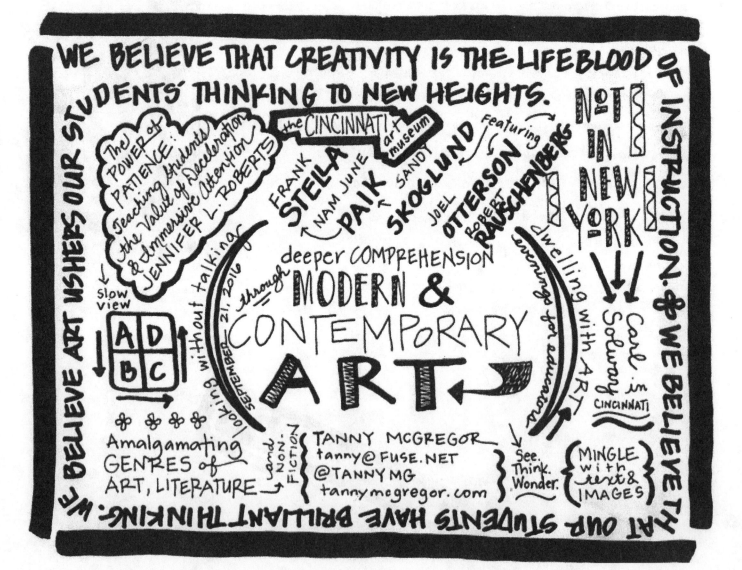

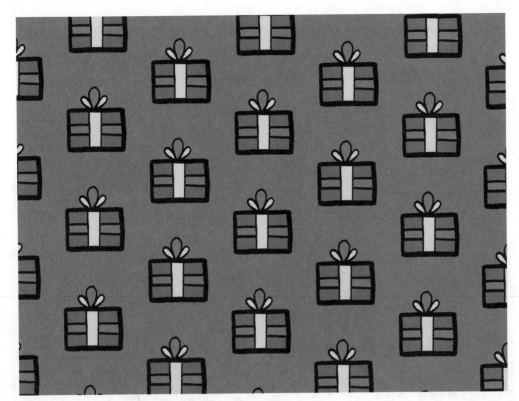

**Digital sketch created with a favorite app, Amaziograph**

## Choosing from the Content Buffet

I'm not generally a fan of restaurant buffets. It's too easy to overload my plate and forget the healthy eating promises I've made to myself. The choices seem endless and I need time to think, but the person behind me is waiting! I guess you could call it buffet line stress, and it's an analogy in the making. When we're reading something complex, listening to a speaker, or even sorting through our own thoughts, it's a lot like walking up to that buffet with empty plate in hand. What do I want on my plate (or my page)? What is better left behind? Should I try something new? Shall I fill the plate now or wait to see what's coming up at the end of the line? It can feel complicated. With your pens or stylus as the utensils to select what you need, let a couple of questions guide you.

57

Ultimately, you need to answer those questions for yourself when you're reading, with or without pen in hand. When sketchnoting, though, it's almost as though you're hyper-metacognitive, with an awareness of the answers to these guiding questions always front and center.

When I'm sketchnoting in a classroom, at a meeting, or during a conference session, students and colleagues have repeatedly asked me: *How do you know what to sketchnote?* Back to the buffet analogy here for a moment. There are certain things for which I'm always on the alert. Take a look at my plate!

**The sketchnote buffet plate, created in Paper by FiftyThree.**

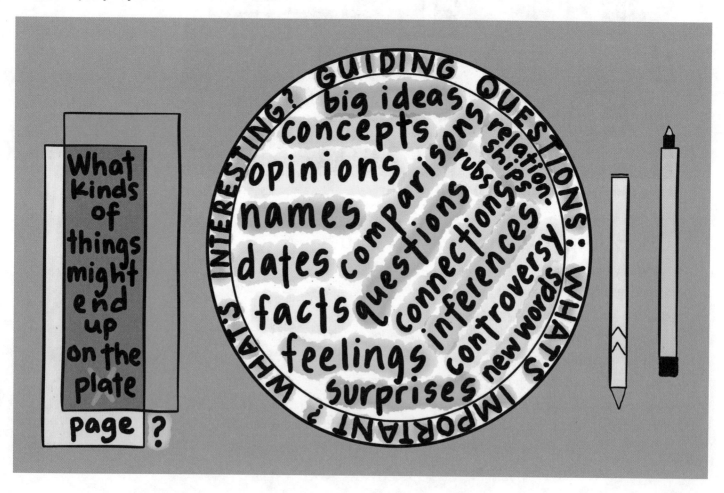

**The beautiful thing about these guiding questions? The answers are all yours.** Yes, there are often similarities between sketchnotes when they share a common textual basis. Individualized responses, though, are what make the sketchnote of value. Take this lesson in a second-grade classroom, for example. When the kids heard the story of Dolly Parton's *Coat of Many Colors* (2016), they were mesmerized. No surprise, since the themes include the importance of family, finding strength against bullies, and how love can make you feel rich. There's a lot to think about in Dolly's story, so of course

The two big questions: *What's important? What's interesting?* Sketchnote created in Paper by FiftyThree.

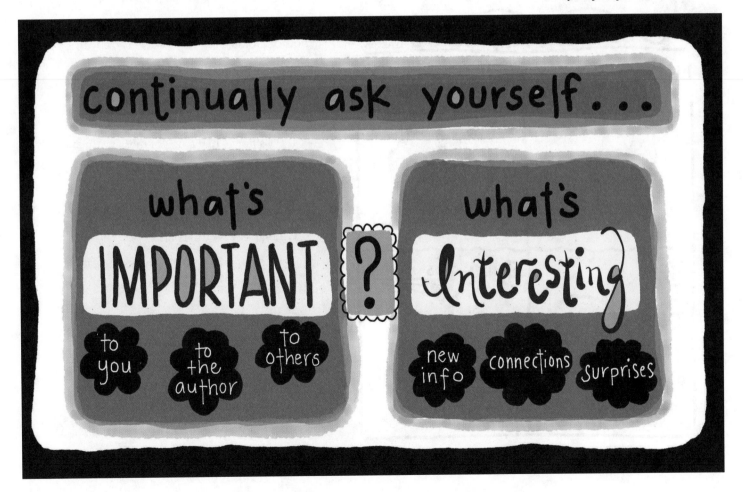

that makes it fertile ground for sketchnoting. In this classroom, we marinated in the text, listening to Dolly sing the story, and then hearing read-alouds of two different picture book versions (same text, different illustrations). With time for talk sprinkled throughout, the kids knew Dolly's story well and had time to reflect a bit before putting marker to paper. We talked together about the big, important parts of Dolly's story. Our thinking frame was this: "What will you remember about Dolly's story? Let's make our invisible thinking show up, like magic, on our pages!" We chunked the story into fourths, giving time for talking and sketching along the way. The big ideas were not lost on these seven-year-olds. In fact, they culled the story for lasting truths as well as anyone could, at any age. As I looked at the sketchnotes appearing on their papers, here's what I saw:

**Dolly's story is told across four quadrants, with each box holding an important idea that the student is not soon to forget.**

- Dolly's family had a box of rags.
- A coat of many colors was pieced together by Dolly's mom.
- The kids at school made fun of Dolly when they saw the coat.
- The coat made Dolly happy because it was made with her mother's love.

A quadrant sketchnote like this one is the beginning of more detailed annotation. Some students were able to show their thinking with words and pictures, others with pictures only. Some sketches were easily decipherable, and others took more time. Each child was able to unpack their thinking in a beautiful, unique fashion, yet the big important ideas showed through clearly. This lesson was memorable because of the way these students were able to make their brilliant thinking visible, one frame at a time. It is always good to think about the work of primary students, regardless of the grade level you teach. Our youngest kids can help us understand where the thinking might go next.

Fast-forward from the primary grades to college for a more detailed example. I recently worked with a group of students from Ohio State University to discuss notetaking habits and to discover the benefits of sketchnoting, specifically with nonfiction reading. We read a variety of informational articles about how moonshiners during Prohibition disguised their footprints by wearing "cow shoes." (Yes, this is true; look it up!) The sketchnotes shown here were created by three students, none majoring in visual art, by the way! There was no talking this time, as the material was read independently and the students sketchnoted what they found to be important and/or interesting.

**Take a moment to study these three sketchnotes. If you have background knowledge about cow shoes, you'll see some confirmations of what you already know. If you've never heard about this strange phenomenon from the 1920s, you'll learn a thing or two and maybe your curiosity will be piqued enough to do a bit of research to answer the questions generated.**

From kindergarten to college, thinking in words and pictures pushes us to intersect with the text, leaving behind unmistakably original sketchnotes.

Remember my friend Karen from the opening story of this chapter? Thanks to friends like her, the details in this chapter came to be. Whether you appreciate the supports outlined here or would rather dive in head first, it's the sketchnoter's thinking that makes all the difference. Rules can feel safe at first, but as your confidence and experience build you will simply *know*. Your gut will be your guide, and you'll become an independent inker.

Chapters 1 through 3 have given you the tools you need to begin sketchnoting and to introduce your students to the practice as well. You can experiment your heart out for weeks and months and years, and, just like me, never tire of visual notetaking. Our thinking can live on in memorable, visual ways of our own creation.

The rest of this book will arm you with sketchnoting ideas to enhance instruction. From the English language arts workshop to the math classroom to the science lab, sketchnotes can contribute to lasting learning across the school day and into the world beyond. If you're still feeling unsure about your own ability to sketchnote well, remember this:

> *"Many of the greatest ideas in business, science and literature have been drawn by people with no formal artistic skill."*
>
> —**Dan Roam, author of *The Back of the Napkin* (2013) and *Draw to Win* (2016)**

Your great ideas, and those of your students, lie ahead.

# Sketching in Science

**Jessica** | K-5 SCIENCE TEACHER

Sketching and drawing are a fundamental part of my elementary science classroom. Most days, at least one of my classes is engaged in representing content visually. Here are a few examples of the ways we've used sketching.

## Observational Drawing

My second-grade students visited our local conservatory earlier this year where they sketched detailed pictures of plants in four different habitats (tropical rain forest, desert, Himalayan mountains, and Pacific island). Back at school, these sketches were used to create murals depicting each habitat. Along with their observations of the temperature and humidity in each room, the murals formed the basis for our study of habitats and adaptations. Meanwhile, my fifth graders measured and sketched owl pellets before dissecting them, and my first-grade students sketched a variety of seeds.

### Sketching to Plan an Experimental Setup or Engineering Design

My fourth-grade students prepared to build hand pollinators by sketching and labeling several designs. They then shared these designs with their partners, discussed them, and settled on one design to build and test. Taking the time to plan through sketching focused their attention and made them more efficient with both time and materials.

### Sketching to Record Results or an Observed Phenomenon

My fourth graders sketch to document the changes they observe in their Wisconsin Fast Plants over their month-long life cycle. Later in the year, they sketch circuits showing which arrangements cause a light bulb to light and which do not. Sometimes, students even draw themselves completing an investigation. What a great example of metacognition in action!

### Sketching to Engage with and Remember Content

When we define a new vocabulary term, students add both a formal definition and a sketch that represents the word's meaning. We also incorporate sketches into notes from videos, class conversations, and text. My third-grade students sketched various types of clouds in a graphic organizer as they read nonfiction text and viewed videos. These sketches are referred to daily as they report on the day's weather to their classmates.

Sketching and drawing certainly add extra time to my lessons and investigations, yet I believe it is a worthwhile trade for several reasons. First, sketching engages students differently than other activities. I have some students who become incredibly more invested in an assignment that allows them to draw and use a variety of colors. It also supports my students who are gaining proficiency with English or who are reluctant writers. These students are often able to communicate their understanding better through a drawing than they are in writing, allowing me to truly assess their learning and not their language proficiency. Sketching also helps my students remember content more

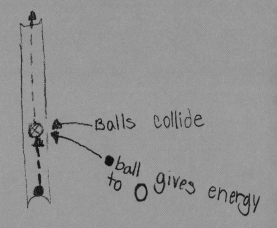

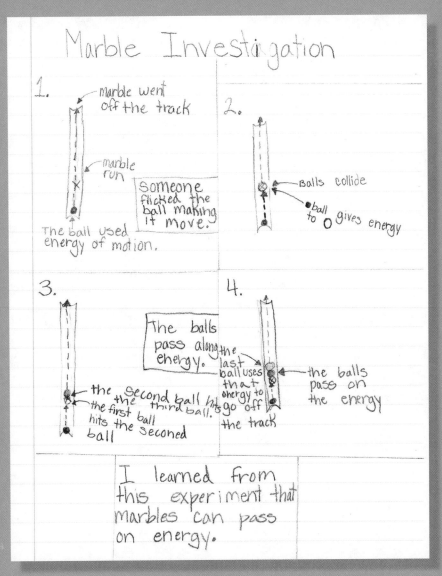

Isabella uses labeled sketches to document her findings while investigating the transfer of energy between marbles.

effectively than writing alone. And finally, sketching mirrors what many scientists do in their daily work. Apprenticing my students into the practices of science is my ultimate goal, and including sketching in my classroom is one way to meet it.

write

nap

daydr

decele

breathe

hike

read

make something

listen to music

exercise

pray

am

ate

watch
the
sky

meditate

@TANNYMCG

garden

doodle

laugh

## CHAPTER 4

# Sketchnote LIVE:
# Be in the Moment

Nearly every day I come across articles about the importance of being present. Titles like *Six Ways to Practice Being Mindful* and *Living in the Here and Now* sometimes draw me in, and I find practical ideas for blocking out the noise of life and moving toward a gratitude mindset, as shown by this background sketchnote. Other times articles like these frustrate me. *Hey, I'm trying to be a wife, mom, friend, and teacher. I'm just surviving here! No time to be bothered with chatter about mindfulness and quiet focus* (the very reason I need it, right?). What I know for sure is that there are so many distracting voices around us, so many forces pulling this way and that. Without a way to settle ourselves and focus (be it through reading, prayer, meditation, exercise, listening to music, etc.), life flies by with less meaning than we deserve. Feel an analogy coming on?

And so it is with *learning* in the moment. If we're not careful, new learning will pass us by. We might be attending a conference keynote address or sitting in an evening graduate class after working all day. In moments like these, social media can call us away from focus, and so can thoughts of life's responsibilities. Likewise, our students might be listening to a read-aloud or viewing a video clip, yet maintaining a focus on new learning is elusive, for reasons too numerous to list here.

Sketchnoting live, in the moment, while listening or reading or viewing, is valuable as we strive for focus to learn something new. Of course sketchnoting can be beneficial for many other reasons specifically named in the first chapter. They are all important. But for this reason alone—a way to find focus—sketchnoting in the moment can stand strong as an instructional approach that deserves a place in our comprehension toolboxes, for our students and ourselves.

Speaking of comprehension, there's something else that happens when we practice sketchnoting live. With every stroke of the pen or stylus, we are exercising metacognitive decision-making. We think about what we hear, see, or read, and tap into the thinking strategies identified by the proficient reader research synthesized by Pearson, Roehler, Dole, and Duffy (1992). We connect with our existing schema. We ask ourselves questions. We determine what is most important. We synthesize information. Our brains are exercised in all of these ways and more. Sketchnoting concretizes the abstract ways our brains make meaning and gives us something visual to show for it.

**Thinking strategy tangram. As we sketchnote, our use of these strategies becomes visible on the page or screen.**

**When we sketchnote live, we are practicing merging our thinking with that of someone (or something) else.** We aren't mindlessly copying what we see. We aren't robotically recording what we hear. We are mining the very essence of meaning in a personalized way, creating a brand-new representation that holds significance for us that is beyond a singular coding system. Words and pictures together encode our thinking, our new learning. So whenever you find yourself or your students with a need to paraphrase or reformulate the ideas of someone else and make them your own, just try live sketchnoting. Don't let new learning pass you by.

## Launching Real-Time Sketchnoting with Your Students

It's a joy to share classroom lesson experiences, but in doing so there's a little bit of fear. I want to provide a sneak peek inside a classroom of sketchnoters, but I don't want you to read for replication. In other words, read and enjoy the classroom glimpse, but don't feel pressured to do it my way. Open up the possibilities for yourself by using a text that feels right for your students. Change up the topic or genre. Whether you choose to use a story, a poem, or a piece of informational text, it's best to go with something that is brief and holds interest for your students. Please don't feel bound by the lesson example that you read here. Replicate or reformulate. It's up to you!

### *Making Something Out of Nothing*

The elementary students look at the blank piece of paper that I hold up. I show them both sides and ask them what they see. "Ummmm . . . nothing?" Tabitha smiles and asks. "You're exactly right! There is no evidence of any thinking . . . yet. So let's change that. Let's read something together and make our thinking visible with sketchnotes. Our thinking is our superpower!" As I

**Materials needed**

Paper or device, colored pencils/pens or stylus, short text or picture book of your choice, and a way to model your own thinking (chart paper, document camera, interactive whiteboard, etc.)

show the cover of *The Little Gift of Nothing* by Patrick McDonnell (2016), I ask the kids to talk about what the title might mean and what they're noticing about the front cover sketch. One student comments that it looks like the author does quick sketches for his illustrations. I remind students that we're going to make our invisible thinking visible and that the representations we create on paper can be a mixture of words and pictures. Some kids take out their sketchmats from the introductory lesson to be reminded of visual features they might want to include in their sketchnotes. "We can sketchnote for many different reasons and at many different times. When you're listening to a read-aloud, you might want to sketchnote to help keep your focus or to remember more of what you're hearing. Part of what you capture on the page could be events or concepts from the story. The other part could be your reactions, connections, or questions to what you're hearing. Try not to limit yourself. If you get stuck, remember our guiding questions: *What's important? What's interesting?* Be open to where the pen takes you. You are about to make something out of nothing!"

I want to make this experience pleasurable and help each sketchnoter to feel supported. Kids might choose to use a windowpane organizer to help move them across the space while we move through the text. Some like the structure that the organizer provides, while others feel more comfortable using the blank space and designing as they go. In either case, we'll stop a few times along the way to take time to think and sketch. I generate a couple of images that I think we'll need while we view the front cover and read the back cover together. "Hmmm. *The Little Gift of Nothing.* I'm going to make a quick idea bank on this chart that we might use as we think about this book. I'm getting these ideas just from looking at the front and back covers. The ideas from this chart are for us to share. Feel free to use them and add to them to make your notes more meaningful." I sketch a couple of images that many kids will want to use and jot down a few key words so kids don't get hung up on spelling the names. "Anyone have anything else to add to the idea bank as we get started?"

**I generated an idea bank, and kids contributed a few questions and even an image to show a "special day." Idea banks give sketchnoters a place to start. Everyone can write or sketch something.**

Will I always create an idea bank when entering into a new sketchnote experience? No. But when many in the group are still on shaky ground, an idea bank can be a welcomed support. Use one when you feel your students could benefit. Soon enough they'll likely be independent enough to dive in on their own.

## Reading and Sketchnoting Together

We begin the text, reading a little, sketching a little. This decelerated pace refreshes me, and I feel the classroom atmosphere relax. There are all kinds of great choices to be made here. You could sketchnote on the whiteboard or on chart paper for your students to see. You could read and walk the room, observing great thinking going on. Your students can talk and sketch in between pages, or sketch in a quiet atmosphere while you read. Take a gallery walk halfway through the book, or wait until the end. Encourage kids to view each other's thinking and think about their own. The important thing is that a great text is shared, new ideas are generated, and visible thinking emerges on the page. In some ways this seems so simple. Read. Think. Sketch. Repeat. But it is a far cry from the deadly "assign and assess" model of reading that pervades so many lessons. It's decelerated. It's thinking-intensive. It's fun. A read-aloud is an ideal time to practice being present with pen in hand. Am I suggesting that kids should sketchnote every time a book is read aloud? No, unless a student chooses to do so because it helps her/him focus and/or understand. What I am suggesting is that the read-aloud is the perfect place to rehearse sketchnoting in the moment—a classroom structure that is already in place where kids can see what it's like to sketchnote live.

**Warner, grade 2, sketchnoted the important things from the story and ended up thinking that the entire book is about love. He generated more images than text here.**

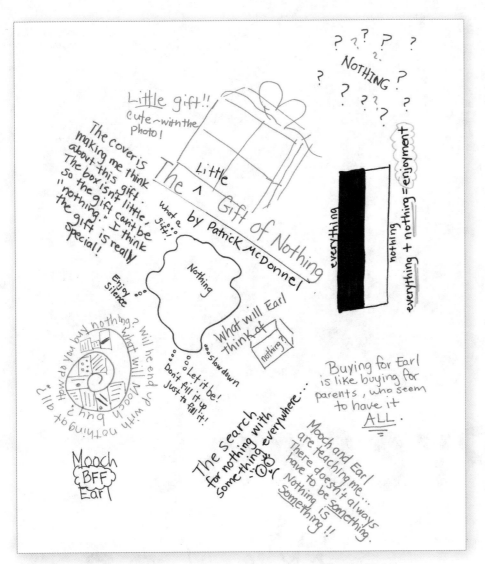

**Karen, a gifted intervention specialist, is most comfortable making her thinking visible with words. In this sketchnote sample, she showed how she is branching out to include colors and symbols to better capture her thoughts.**

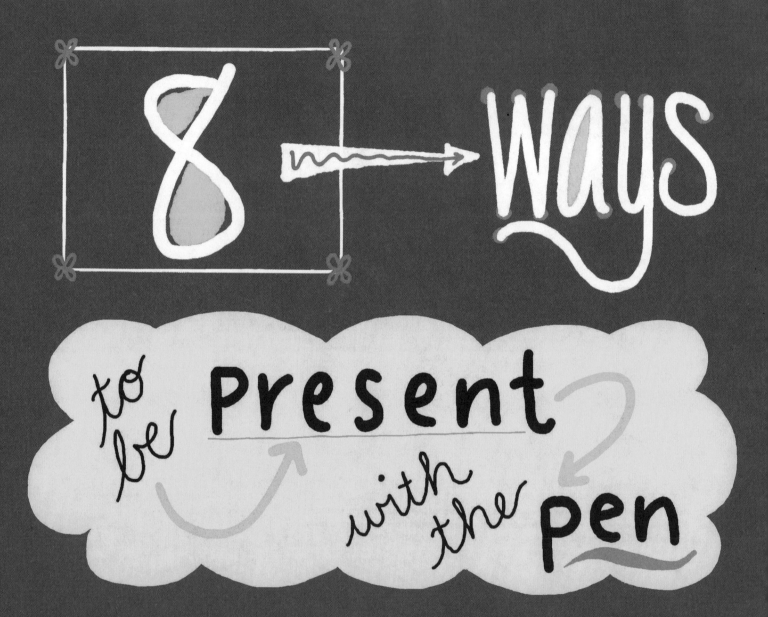

8 ways to be present with the pen

READ-
ALOUD

MUSIC

AUDIO
CONTENT

DAILY
SKETCH

Opportunities for sketchnoting in real
time happen all through the day. Used
as an instructional approach in the body
of a lesson or fit in around the edges of
your day, sketchnoting live can deepen
understanding while helping kids become
*decelerated readers*. Check out the
following ideas for sketchnoting live,
complete with samples from sketchnoters
of all ages. Pick and choose. Enjoy.

TEXT
EXCERPTS

IMAGES &
OBJECTS

MARGINALIA

DIRECT
INSTRUCTION

# SKETCHNOTE
↳ *live* during a READ-ALOUD

## ACCESS
to → materials:
Sketchbooks
devices
pens & paper
markers, etc.

DAILY PRACTICE

any
genre

Students choose to S K E T C H (or not)

Show your THINKING

mix of words & pictures

VISUALIZE 👁

{ it's calming }

IMPROVE listening COMPREHENSION

READ-ALOUD

**Third-grader Harmony sketched and wrote while listening to *Charlotte's Web.* Notice how many character traits materialized on the page: kind, helpful, success(ful), polite, determined, loyal. She also captured interesting words, phrases, and sentences, sprinkling them around the page as she listened.**

**Maeve, grade 5, sketchnoted as she listened to a class read-aloud. *The Last Fifth Grade of Emerson Elementary* comes to life on the page with Maeve's use of color and arrows, but it's the mix of quick phrases and questions that let us know she is thinking with pens as the story unfolds.**

79

# SKETCHNOTE L, live while listening to 🎼 MUSIC

## LISTEN for REPETITION

**the LYRICS → are the text**

consider printing or projecting LYRICS

TRY → MANY GENRES.

to DETERMINE BIG IDEAS

HOW MANY STUDENTS do you have?

EXPERIMENT with INSTRUMENTAL *music*

what comes to mind?

PLAY → IT → AGAIN

RE-listening IS RE-reading

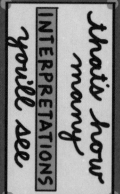

that's how many INTERPRETATIONS you'll see

This sketchnote was created by Geovanny, a musician. He listened to Dave Brubeck's jazz standard, *Blue Rondo à la Turk* while it played on repeat, allowing the colors and shapes to show what he saw in his mind. Sparse on text, rich in color and texture, Geo's work reminds us that sometimes thinking doesn't emerge linguistically on the page. It should be honored as thinking, just the same.

Susan, a university professor, sketchnoted as she listened to *Windmills of Your Mind*. She captured figurative phrases from the lyrics that referenced ripples, tunnels, clocks, wheels, and balloons, and paired them with simple symbols. Susan listened to the song once without pen in hand, then listened two more times as she created a visual representation of Sting's interpretation of this beautiful melody.

# SKETCHNOTE → live / as AUDIO CONTENT plays

- Podcasts
- TED talks
- Audiobooks
- Newscasts
- Speeches
- Keynotes
- Poetry
- Radio Shows ↘ (old & new)

SINCE THERE IS NO VISUAL, **make your own.**

SO MUCH CONTENT OUT THERE! ↘

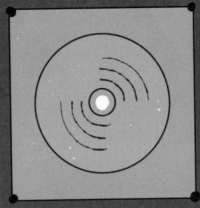

STOP → the audio for *extra* TALK or SKETCH time.

DISCOVER your inner SYNESTHETE.

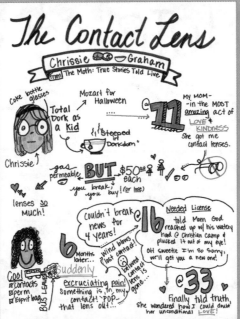

Johnny, a learning design specialist listened to an audio story as he sketchnoted. He told me later that he had so many connections to this story that the words and pictures flowed easily from the pens. He relived his story as he listened to the experience of another. Listen to "The Contact Lens" and other interesting stories like these at www.themoth.org.

Angela, a secondary literacy coach, sketchnoted as she listened to *The Coaching Habit Podcast* (www.boxofcrayons.com). This particular episode featured author Jim Knight's "one best question."

So many ideas on a single page. Valinda, a reading specialist, listened to a TED Talk and sketchnoted while she learned. *The Power of Vulnerability*, like so many TED Talks, is loaded with layered concepts and moves at a fast pace. Valinda determined what was most important to her and recorded her thinking in a spatial way that is clear and interesting.

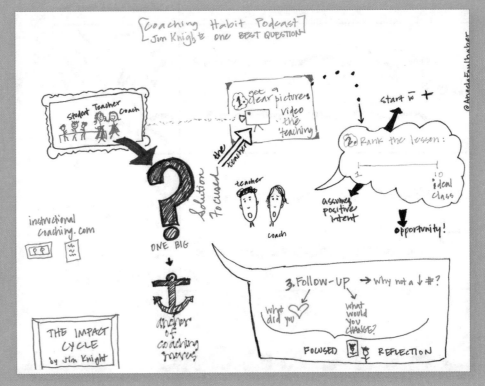

AUDIO CONTENT

# SKETCHNOTE ↳ *live* with TEXT EXCERPTS

## READ CLOSELY & DEEPLY with ↳ PEN in HAND

Chunk text into pieces.

☀ 🌥 humidity

🌴 heat

🌧 rainfall

CORRESPONDING SKETCHES

COMPLEX *text* ?
Abstract ?
DENSE or UNFRIENDLY ?

✳ Sketchnote *to* UNDERSTAND.

Third-graders Logan and Finola sketchnoted from a text excerpt about the Mississippi River. Although they both read the same text, their sketchnotes show different points of interest. Logan was fascinated by the journey that water takes from the source to the mouth of the river. Finola couldn't believe how deep the Mississippi can be when it reaches Louisiana!

TEXT EXCERPTS

# SKETCHNOTE ↳ live

at the time of

# DIRECT INSTRUCTION

→ fight DISTRACTION & BOREDOM !

## STAY focused → DURING

| lectures | conferences |
|----------|-------------|
| sermons | mini-lessons |
| workshops | instructions |

capture BIG ideas & **little points of INTEREST**

Compensate for a **SHORT ATTENTION SPAN**

Jasmine, a high school junior, viewed PowerPoint slides that her teacher had prepared. She captured sequenced information with phrases and symbols, letting go of the urgency to copy from each slide.

We all know how many notes are taken in undergraduate education programs as we prepare to become teachers. Kayla, a first-year education major, has already found a way to make her notes her own. Using different lettering styles and visual features, she kept pace with the information presented without getting bogged down with detailed drawings.

**DIRECT INSTRUCTION**

# SKETCHNOTE live

*when creating* → MARGINALIA

aka "tracks *in the* snow" & "footprints *in the* sand"

\* USE ANY AND ALL? available space.

It's all up to you.

Enter into a "SKETCHY" dialogue *with the* AUTHOR

Sketch-notes CAN BE *more* **meaningful** than ↙↓ using a HIGH-LIGHTER

When you can't write in the text,

\* & + ! • CODE THE TEXT ? :) # >< 

*you create the* CODE!

sticky notes → *are a* Sketchnoter's FRIEND.

MARGINALIA

Fourth-grade sketchnoter Tallulah used a triple-column organizer to think her way through chunks of text. The first column includes the text itself. The second and third columns, shown here, are where she added quick symbols to help her code her emotions and connections, and small sketchnotes to elaborate on her thinking.

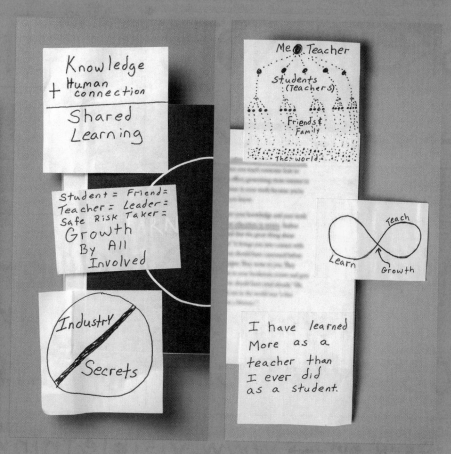

These two photos show how science teacher Matt left behind tracks of his thinking when he read. Matt used equations, symbols, and models, as well as conventionally structured language, to capture his takeaways and solidify his new learning. No rules. He jotted down his thinking in the way that worked best for him.

# SKETCHNOTE ↳ *live*

*while viewing* & **IMAGES OBJECTS**

MAKE → *detailed* OBSERVATIONS

CreaTe *unique* INTERPRETATIONS

↝CHECK OUT→ www.visiblethinkingpz.org

SKETCH [what you] SEE. Think. Wonder.

DWELL *longer*

&

learn to REALLY SEE

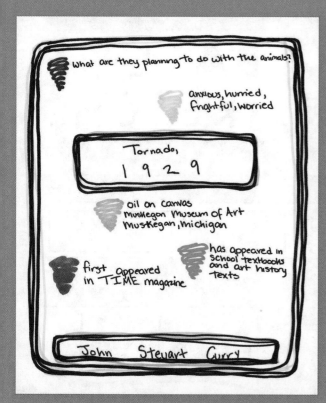

Cassida created notecards to save her thinking about images viewed. Here she used a bit of color and a repeating image to help her remember a few interesting facts, along with a question and a few emotions the people in the painting seem to be feeling.

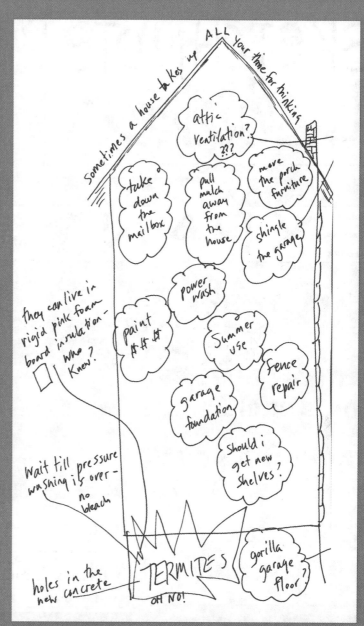

Angela sat inside her aging garage and considered what it might take to turn it into a usable structure. Her sketchnote was created as she spent time looking at the original 1926 construction, letting her pen record possibilities, drawbacks, and observations. Being in the space, in the moment, helped the sketchnote take shape.

IMAGES & OBJECTS

# SKETCHNOTE ↳ live & create a

## DAILY SKETCH

## EXPAND your VISUAL LEXICON

### Sketch HERE:

* interactive notebooks
* morning pages
* gratitude journals

## MAKE creativity

PART of your everyday ROUTINE

**be NONJUDGMENTAL**
with yourself & others
QUICK SKETCHES, NOT MASTERPIECES

**Challenge → YOURSELF →**
(5 minutes, tops)

to a *daily* DRAW

A sketchnoted page from Blythe's gratitude journal shows what she was thankful for. This is called a "What Went Well" or "Three Blessings" exercise. Psychologist and author Martin Seligman writes about the benefits of keeping such a daily journal. Blythe's entries are quick and simple and chronicle the good in her life.

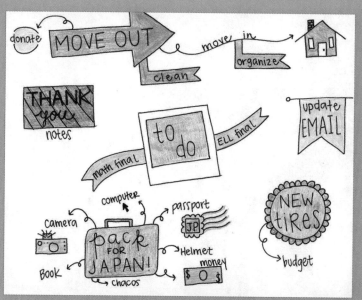

Claire, a college junior, creates sketchnotes for professional and personal reasons. On this page, she created a visual to-do list for the end-of-year time crunch, which included exams, a move, and an upcoming mission trip. Sketchnoting allowed her to slow down, sift through muddled thinking, and decide what was important moving forward.

**DAILY SKETCH**

There are so many ways to sketchnote in the moment . . . so many ways to make thinking visible, visual, and meaningful. I've mentioned but a few. Try these for yourself to begin a journey of self-discovery. Try these with your students to open up a window into their brilliant minds.

# Sketchnoting for Reading Comprehension

### Lauren | THIRD-GRADE TEACHER

My students have become enthusiastic sketchnoters and are eager to illustrate their thinking about their reading in this unique way.

I especially appreciate that sketchnoting is accessible to all learners. English language learners and striving readers in my classroom have been able to demonstrate their understanding through sketchnoting in small groups and in independent reading. Although they may not comprehend a reading passage in its entirety, they can identify what they *do* understand and illustrate it. This provides them a point of entry into difficult text that may have previously been intimidating for them.

Sketchnoting has also has been a wonderful way for me to quickly assess a student's understanding of a text. The words and images they choose to include after reading provide insight into their level of comprehension. I have also integrated sketchnoting into texts students read at

Lauren's students create quick sketches that fit into the margins of the page. Small symbols and words or phrases help her students make their thinking visible and easy to share. Kids can quickly recall their thinking when they glance back at what they sketched from the day before.

home. I ask them to sketchnote at specific points in passages to encourage them to monitor their own comprehension.

Sketchnoting has helped the text come alive for readers in my classroom.

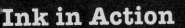 

# Sketchnoting to Empower Striving Readers

**Kara** | SEVENTH- AND EIGHTH-GRADE
INTERVENTION SPECIALIST

This year, I taught my eighth-grade reading intervention students some sketch-noting techniques. As we read Sara Pennypacker's *Pax* as part of The Global Read Aloud, I asked my students to sketchnote as they read. They blew me away. Students who would stare at me blankly when asked to discuss a chapter were suddenly not only able to discuss the book but articulate their under-standings and insights.

Sketchnoting is a practice that will stay with me—I now use it as a method of learning myself.

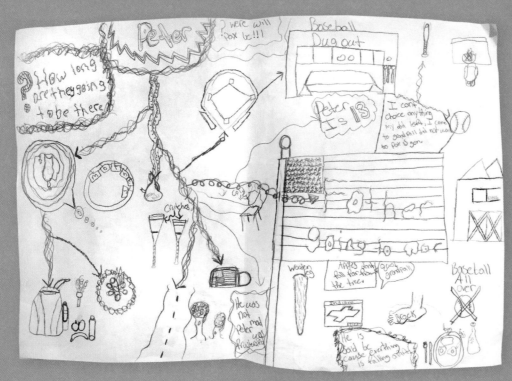

Deaton made these sketchnotes while reading *Pax*. He said that he had never thought of himself as an artist, but after our work with sketchnoting, he became interested in taking art as an elective.

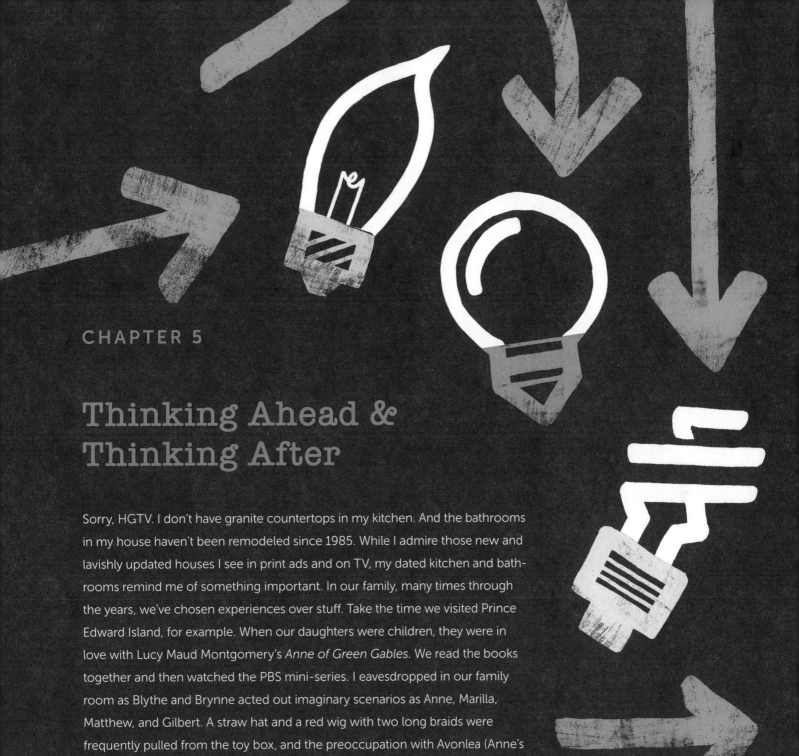

## CHAPTER 5

# Thinking Ahead & Thinking After

Sorry, HGTV. I don't have granite countertops in my kitchen. And the bathrooms in my house haven't been remodeled since 1985. While I admire those new and lavishly updated houses I see in print ads and on TV, my dated kitchen and bathrooms remind me of something important. In our family, many times through the years, we've chosen experiences over stuff. Take the time we visited Prince Edward Island, for example. When our daughters were children, they were in love with Lucy Maud Montgomery's *Anne of Green Gables*. We read the books together and then watched the PBS mini-series. I eavesdropped in our family room as Blythe and Brynne acted out imaginary scenarios as Anne, Marilla, Matthew, and Gilbert. A straw hat and a red wig with two long braids were frequently pulled from the toy box, and the preoccupation with Avonlea (Anne's home) went on and on, long after I expected it to be replaced by some other childhood fascination.

What does this have to do with my ugly old kitchen and bathrooms? Everything.

Our family decided to visit Prince Edward Island, the setting for Anne's adventures, and use our money for an experience that would surface in our family's conversations forever. So we saved. We made sacrifices. And when the time came to figure out the travel arrangements, our outdated house and what we did without seemed insignificant. This decision was the first of many where we opted for doing something together instead of buying something together.

I had a realization when planning that family trip. We were already enjoying the trip months before we ever left home. The nightly dinner table conversation.

The collecting of travel tips from friends who had already visited this province of Canada. The PEI brochures we poured over, as we looked for a cottage and places to hike. Half of the fun was in organizing our plans, preparing ourselves for time away together. I even devoted a page in my sketchbook to our PEI vacation on the night we decided to book the flights. Thinking ahead was not only pleasurable but pragmatic. Our thinking ahead helped us more easily make decisions while in PEI because we had done our research. Thinking *ahead* is worth it!

After the trip was over, I again realized something interesting. As time passed, we continued to have those dinner table conversations about PEI. Even today, almost ten years later, great memories about our PEI experience punctuate our lives and are lasting treasures because we not only experienced life in PEI but we reflected on it regularly upon our return home. The reflection, although after the fact, boosts the meaningfulness of the actual experience. Thoughtful reflection takes an experience and makes it lasting and memorable. It allows us to relive the experience over and over again in our minds. Thinking *after* is worth it.

You probably see where I'm going with this. As we enter into a learning experience (a professional learning workshop, a keynote address, the reading of text), we don't have to wait for the learning to start. Grab your notebook or device and begin to "preflect." What do you already know? What questions do you have going in? How will you organize your thinking during the experience? Likewise, after experiencing the learning (through listening, reading, writing, viewing, etc.), grab your notebook or device and reflect in a visible, even sharable way. If the question is how to think more deeply about an experience (whether it be reading or otherwise), then one answer is sketchnoting. We can learn before, during, and after. We can prepare, organize, and reflect with our sketchnotes.

Chapter 4's focus was the experience of sketchnoting while learning. This chapter looks at the ahead-of-time sketchnotes that you and your students might create to prepare for what's to come and organize your thinking. It also includes the after-the-fact sketchnotes that can be designed with metacognitive thought and reflection. Ahead and after. Preflection and reflection. Getting our brains ready, then sealing the deal with rich thought put into action.

**Materials needed**

Pens/stylus, t-chart in notebook or journal (paper or digital), a curiosity about something new for you or your students, and resources where you and/or your students can meet new information

## Launching the Schema Sketch with Your Students

If you're like me, you sometimes think you can solve all of the world's problems with a t-chart. The good old t-chart is ideal for a schema sketch, the perfect before-and-after tool. It's a simple way to show students how much their thinking has grown, right before their eyes.

Here's a peek inside a discovery experience with a group of students who don't know much about paleontologist Mary Anning . . . yet!

### What Did You Know and What Did You Learn?

"We're soon going to be reading about an important person in history that you might not know much about. That will soon change, though, as we cover some new territory together, reading and viewing about her fascinating, curious life. Let's try something called a schema sketch. It's pretty basic, just a t-chart with labels at the top of each column. On the left, we'll use words and pictures to show what we know right now, our current schema. Then we'll let some time pass. We'll look at her portrait, read some short pieces of informational text with images, and talk together a lot. Eventually we'll return to our schema sketch chart to show our new learning! We can put this page into your notebooks to show what you know now and how much your thinking will grow over time. The topic? Mary Anning." As I announce the topic, some kids seem enthusiastic, others look unsure. These responses likely have to do with how much background knowledge each student thinks they have . . . or lack.

"Never heard of her."

"I know about her! There's a SciShow video about her on YouTube."

"I have no clue."

"Didn't we read about her in *Storyworks*?"

I tell the students, "No shame, no blame. If you know quite a bit about Mary, that's good! If you don't have much prior knowledge about her, that's all right, too! In fact, if you don't know much about this topic, you'll stand to learn a lot. It's exciting either way." I distribute a simple graphic organizer to each student. "When you're ready, go ahead and make your schema visible in the left column. What do you already know, or think you know, about Mary? Use a combination of words and pictures to share your thinking. If you don't know anything at all about her, you can use the first column to make a guess, ask a question, or simply write that you aren't familiar with her story."

When the left side of the t-chart has been completed, we put the papers aside. Now it's time to try to satisfy our building curiosity about Mary Anning. We hold fossils (found in the woods behind my house) in our hands. Next I project images about Mary, and the students talk about each one for a couple of minutes: a portrait of Mary, photographs of the Lyme Regis coast where she lived, sketches of some of the creatures' bones Mary uncovered. We watch a video clip about Mary's life and have a time to "mingle" with text snippets and images. All of this is accomplished without me saying much at all—it's the students who are building background knowledge with each other, independently. A lot of student-to-student talk makes this work. When the time is right, we revisit our schema sketches.

I remind the kids, "Only a short time ago, many of you did not know much, if anything, about fossil hunter Mary Anning. With the help of your friends and a few images and resources, though, you've built some knowledge about her that you can share. Let's go back to our schema sketch pages and take a look at the right side. It's time to show your new learning! Use words and symbols to show what you now know."

In spite of its simplicity, the schema sketch serves several purposes. It allows for metacognitive thought about what is known and what is yet

### What do I already know about Mary Anning?

When creating a schema sketch, some students might not have background knowledge about the topic. This student used sketchnoting to playfully note that this is a new topic for him. You can also invite students to ask questions or make comments about where they are right now.

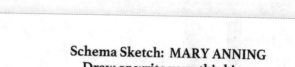

### Schema Sketch: MARY ANNING
#### Draw or write your thinking.

| What do I already know about Mary Anning? | What is my new learning about her? |
|---|---|

Students can choose how to show information on the right side of a schema sketch. Simple, sketchnoted elements help students unveil their new learning.

to be known. It encourages student individuality and choice. And maybe most importantly, it allows students to see their thinking grow and change over time.

Any time you're introducing students to new content, a schema sketch can be a valuable tool. I've used it with third graders at the beginning of a unit about rocks, with intermediate students before reading *Number the Stars* by Lois Lowry, and with social studies teachers before exploring the effects of the Dust Bowl. I've also used the structure and process of a schema sketch in my personal notebooks. I've found them to be an easy way to see where I am and what I know at the moment, and then to capture new learning right there in the same spot. One page. Amazing changes. Take this example. My friend Aidelina gave me a plate of tamales for a holiday gift. I had heard that she was a great

cook but had never tasted any of her creations. I did not know what was inside tamales or how to eat them or if I could freeze the leftovers. In my sketchbook I made a t-chart (a bit lopsided since I knew less at first that I was sure to learn later) and filled the left side with what I knew about tamales, which wasn't much. Didn't they have something to do with corn or cornhusks? Isn't there a story in my picture book collection about a girl who loses her mother's ring in a batch of tamales? Aidelina gave the plate of tamales to me but I didn't get a chance to ask her any questions. For this schema sketch, I added a narrow column in the middle of the chart to show what I did do to learn more. I talked to her son, I watched a couple of YouTube videos about how to make and eat tamales, and I read an article about the best restaurant tamales available in Cincinnati. Now, thanks to Aidelina's delicious gift, I know so much. The most important new learning? Don't eat the cornhusk wrapper. I might have learned that the hard way.

Besides schema sketches, what else can we do to help our students and ourselves think and sketch ahead and after? There are endless possibilities, but the following pages show some great options for getting started.

## Think Ahead with a Visual K-W-L Chart

I remember using K-W-L charts during my first year in the classroom, nearly thirty years ago. The structure helped guide my thoughts as I helped students guide theirs. In 1986, Donna M. Ogle shared this way of organizing with the literacy community, and her three-column organizer has been included in countless lessons since then. We can expand the use of K-W-L charts when we welcome color, symbols, and sketches into the columns. Andrea, a middle school teacher, encourages her students to create visual K-W-L charts when preparing to read about an unfamiliar topic, especially when students may have questions or misconceptions to clear up.

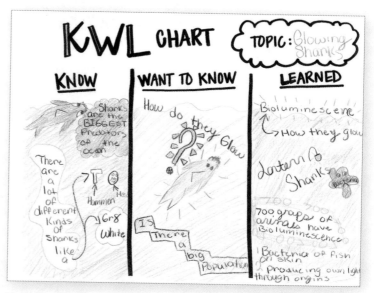

Notice how Shelby already had some general knowledge about sharks before reading but learned some specialized information along the way. Her questions guided her learning, and her sketchnotes are likely to help her remember it.

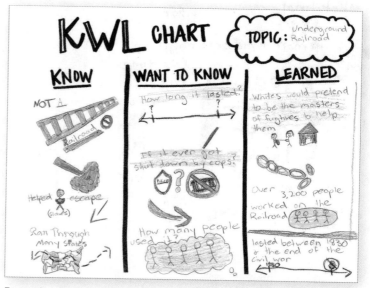

For each column in the K-W-L chart, Annelise created captioned symbols to clearly communicate her thinking. It is easy to see exactly what she knows and wonders.

# Think Ahead with Idea Banks

An idea bank serves as a repository for words, thoughts, questions, and more. Also known as "idea floods," these compilations can be anything from grocery lists to collections of potential research topics. When we expand this tool to include sketchnotes, we're able to decelerate our planning processes and allow our ideas to flow freely.

Thomas kept track of vocabulary words in a visual dictionary. This bank of new words helped him jog his memory and hold on to meanings longer.

**Right after my session proposal was accepted for the International Literacy Association Conference, I made a quick sketchnote in my notebook so I wouldn't forget how I wanted the session to go.**

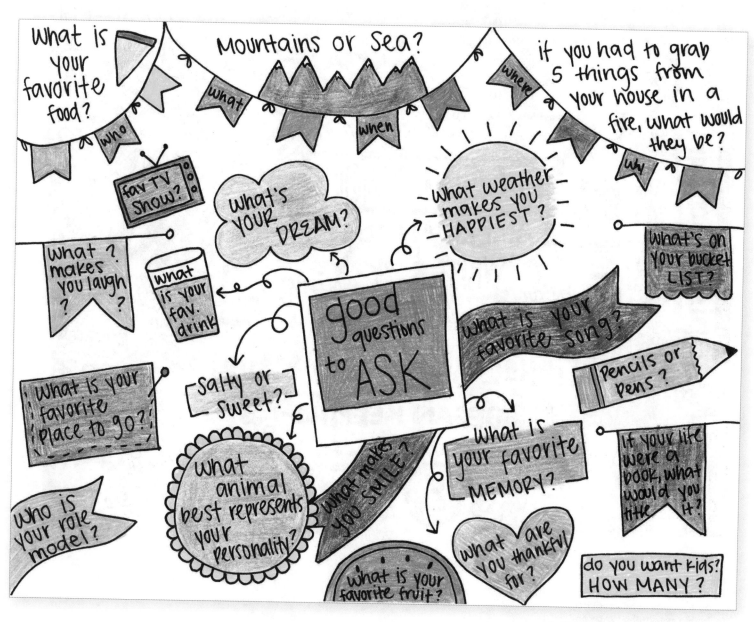

As Claire began her student-teaching assignment, she captured a collection of questions that she might ask her students to get to know them better.

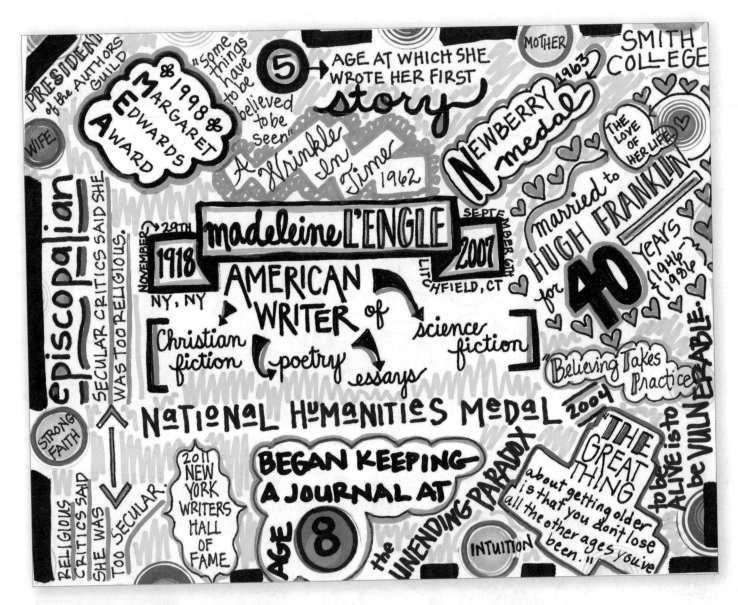

I couldn't love author Madeleine L'Engle more. One evening I grabbed my notebook and created an idea flood about her, including everything I knew and admired. I plan to write about Madeleine one day and will use this sketchnote when I do.

# Think After with a Symbol Sketch

Our youngest readers often enjoy rebus stories, with symbols inserted into the text to support meaning-making. Too often we think of these symbols as a temporary scaffold that we should discard as readers progress in their ability to decode. The irony is that symbols hold meaning . . . a lot of meaning. Humans have communicated this way since the beginning of time. Why not continue using symbols as the depth of thinking becomes more sophisticated? Why let go of symbols at all?

**When thinking about possible themes in literature, symbols can help the reader quickly catch and record an idea. Here Anna thought about the characters in *The Outsiders* by S. E. Hinton with colorful pictures for the big ideas and words when clarification was necessary.**

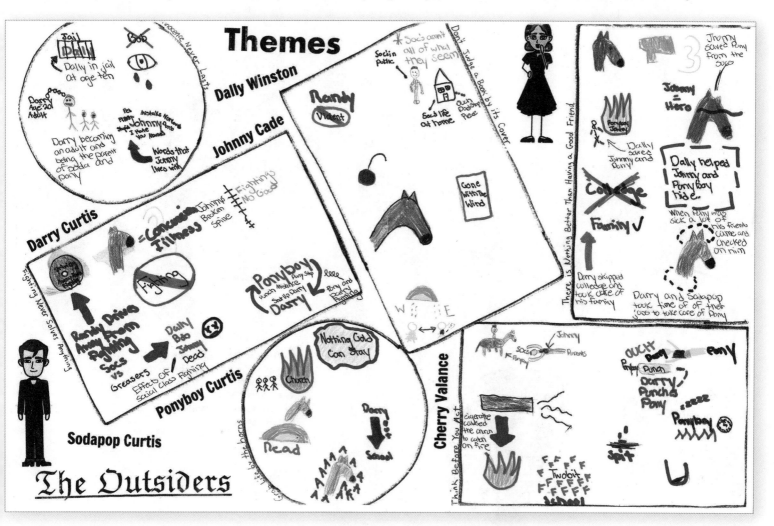

111

## Think After to Summarize and Synthesize

Many teachers agree that teaching summarizing and synthesizing is not an easy or straightforward task. It involves a nuanced combination of skills, strategies, and the reader's own thinking, distilled into a rich, meaning-packed concentrate. The use of sketchnotes can help. By widening the options readers have to express their thinking, we welcome their syntheses without limitation.

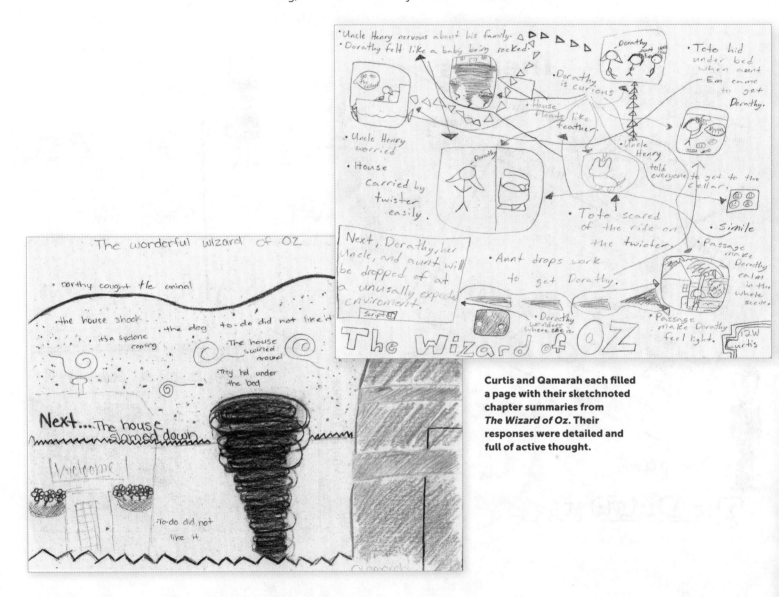

**Curtis and Qamarah each filled a page with their sketchnoted chapter summaries from *The Wizard of Oz*. Their responses were detailed and full of active thought.**

Intermediate students Brynn, Kayley, Monica, and Tommy created sketchnoted book jackets of favorite reads to keep in their notebooks. Intentional selection of important symbols shows up in these remixes.

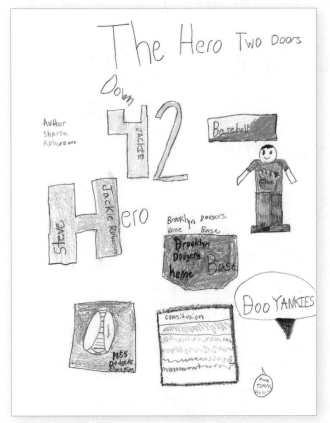

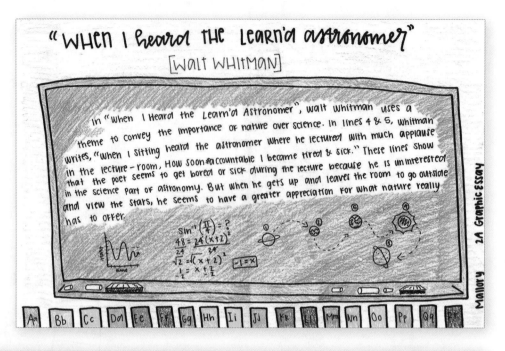

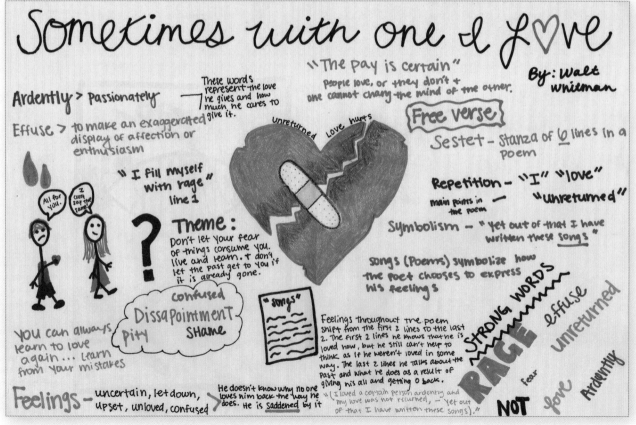

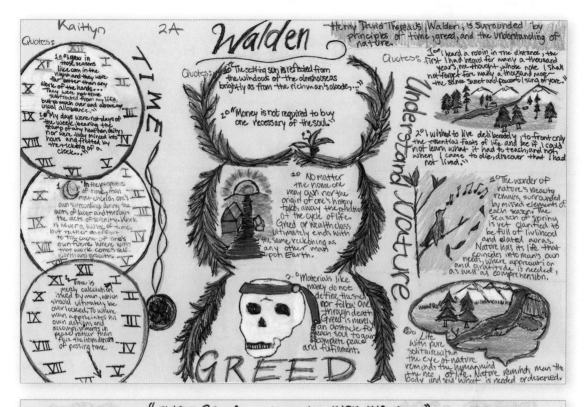

Buffy's high school students created beautiful, unique interpretations of poetry through ample opportunities to read, talk, and sketchnote. In these graphic essays created by Mallory, Leyla, and Kaitlyn, art *and* thinking are synthesized, and both are valued in this idea-rich English language arts class.

## Think After with Daily Reflections

Reflecting can help us to solidify what we've learned, to consider what matters most to us, and to be metacognitive. Yet, reflection time can easily feel teacher-centric (if it involves prompts) or under-structured (if it is offered as a vague invitation). Perhaps this is why it is often the first thing to be eliminated when schedules get tight and time runs out. Sketchnoting our reflections gives us a clear repeatable protocol that honors individual learners' insights.

**Homeschooled students Luke and Sophie made notebook entries at day's end to reflect upon the best things that happened to them. A series of these reflections created a visual diary to hold memories otherwise lost.**

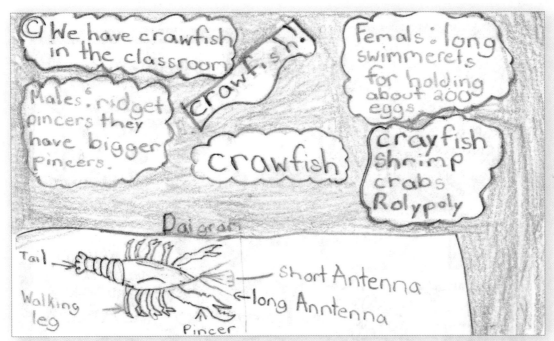

In Cassy's third-grade classroom, students made exit tickets to synthesize their learning at the end of a lesson. These weren't just typical exit tickets, though. Sketchnoting allowed for greater expression and shareability. Here Jaxon and Andres showed what they learned about crayfish and influenza, respectively.

**After a day of coaching, I sometimes sit down after dinner to relax with my notebook and pens. Here's what was on my mind one August evening, after an initial visit with a classroom of first graders.**

So many ideas to try! Where can you begin? When thinking about a lesson plan, ask yourself, "Is there a place in this lesson where students can opt to use non-linguistic representation along with or in lieu of conventional writing, should they so choose? Can the way we use classroom time show that we value the process of sketchnoting, in and of itself? How and when might students decide to share their visual thinking?" This chapter stands as a reminder that sketchnoting doesn't require adding more to our instructional overload, but instead allows us to substitute the choice and creativity that conventional response options sometimes do not inspire. Ahead of time and after the learning, let them think with ink.

# Sketchnoting in High School

## Lisa | HIGH SCHOOL ENGLISH TEACHER

I first used sketchnoting in the classroom with my grade 9 English class. After the class experimented with fonts, bullets, people, and frames on a template, I read an article aloud on Navajo code talkers. Although the article aligned with our thematic unit, students did not have background knowledge on the topic. I was very curious to see what they would come up with. Interestingly, a few of the stronger readers had a harder time using pictures and tended to use more words. The remaining students, including those who struggle with reading, filled their boxes with pictures. After the reading, the students were able to retell the story in pairs in great detail.

Next, the students sketchnoted to brainstorm for writing their own autobiographies. You could hear a pin drop while they were thinking and drawing! When they began typing their autobiography, the students kept their journals in front of them, checking off the pictures as they wrote.

I have since tried sketchnoting with my grade 10 English and grade 11 history classes. I find students are more comfortable drawing pictures because they do not worry about spelling, nor are they concerned about proper structure while they focus their listening and thinking. Students who have trouble with fine motor skills also find sketchnoting easier: They don't have to worry about the neatness of their writing because the work is for their own learning. Weeks later, the students were still able to retell the plot or the ideas of a text, by just looking at their sketchnote page. I have also found that it gives all learners an outlet for their thinking, whether it be in a random all-over-the-page style or a more linear, organized fashion. Finally, students saw that it is okay to take risks; that's how we learn!

(Left) Trina sketchnoted in response to a narrative essay about explorer Ernest Shackleton that was read aloud to the class. She then used these sketchnotes to help recall details as she engaged in conversation with her partner.

(Right) As part of a thematic unit called "The Hero's Journey," Taylor sketchnoted as she read, listened, and talked with her classmates. Notice the detail she was able to capture on one page.

Overall, I have found the majority of my students enjoy the sketchnoting process. A few still prefer using words or taking standard notes, but for many, it gives the students an alternative way to show their thinking. Students have commented favorably on the flexibility of sketchnoting, ("I can include what I want to include" and "[it's] up to you to decide what was important"), the tone of the lesson ("the lesson seemed more relaxed and wasn't so formal like when we take notes"), and the final product ("it looked cool"). I will continue to provide sketchnoting as a strategy and learning opportunity in all my classes.

## CHAPTER 6

# Sketchnote Tapas

If you read Chapter 3, you
already know I don't love buffets.
The idea of sampling new foods and
enjoying a variety of flavors *does* appeal to me, just not in a buffet line. Enter
tapas! A little bit of this and a little bit of that. These small plates originated in
Spanish cuisine, but the experience of sampling many foods, as appetizers or
full meals, has reached into countries and cultures around the world. Having
dinner at the tapas bar near my house always feels exciting. My husband, Miles,
and I can take a chance and order a new dish for just a few dollars. If we like
it, we might discover a wonderful new meal idea, new flavor, or new cuisine. If
we don't like it, there's always another tapa on the menu. Sampling tapas gives
us a reason to try a little bit of everything. Adventurous eating.

This chapter is like a menu of sketchnoting tapas, with appetizer ideas that allow you and your students to sample the joys of sketchnoting to see what is useful and meaningful to you. Perhaps you don't have time for a full-on sketchnoting lesson but still want to give students a chance for creative, nonlinguistic expression. Or maybe there are occasions when your students respond in traditional ways, and some sketchnoting added to the mix might make things more exciting. The ideas shared here will help you integrate sketchnoting into your everyday life, personally and professionally. Whatever the case, take a look at the sketchnote tapas here, to taste and enjoy at will. The sketchnoted thinking you'll find here varies from student- and teacher-

**This example from my digital notebook was a variation of a classroom message I shared with students for many years. While the motto itself may seem like very simple text, the ideas that collaboration and joy are central to learning are transformative. The colorful symbols and playful nature of the images help to convey that joy and collaboration are central to our work, not just pleasantries.**

created samples to pages from my own notebooks. I hope that the tapas in this chapter will not only be delicious on their own but will also spark ideas for you about new ways to use sketchnotes.

## Sketchnoting to Connect to Ideas

Complex ideas can be tough to communicate, and our responses to them might be complex as well. Visual representations can help us to hold on to ideas *and* to integrate our perspective with the ideas. The following examples show you how.

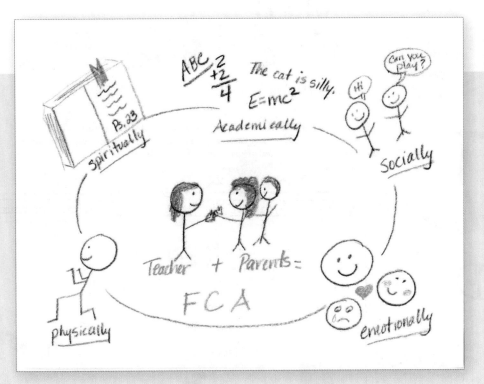

Laura, an elementary principal, asked teachers to create a visual from their school's mission statement, showing as much as they could remember without looking. First-grade teacher Cheri's sketchnote captures the big concepts at this religious academy in simple ways.

**try this**

Sketchnote your district, school, or classroom vision or mission statement.

**try this**

Create a sketchnote based on a thought-provoking quotation.

**High school sketchnoter Maddy melds a few quotations lifted from _Romeo and Juliet_ and a few of her own takeaways and insights from her reading to convey what is meaningful to her about Act II, Scene iii.**

**Middle school ELA teacher Andrea creates "sketchquotes" to elicit responses about the text, to model sketchnoting techniques for her students, and to show how she values students' thinking.**

**Fifth grader Abby loves cats! Here she made a quick sketchnote to illustrate a quotation about her favorite topic. The quote, some symbols, and a few words were all she needed.**

## Sketchnoting to Synthesize What We've Learned

When we've learned a lot of new information, we have a choice to make. We can rely on our memories and hope for the best, or we can make the invisible visible. A sketchnoted synthesis helps us hold on to new learning longer. We can do this in practical ways, as you'll see here.

**try this**

Encourage students to sketch as they study content or even to create sketchnote study guides.

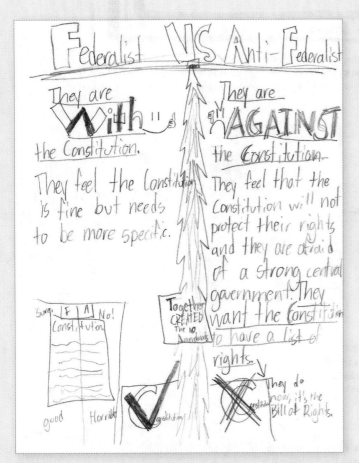

**Fifth grader Reagan prepared for an upcoming social studies quiz by organizing information and studies with pencil in hand.**

**Undergraduate film student Brynne created visual study sheets as she learned new content in a French cinema course.**

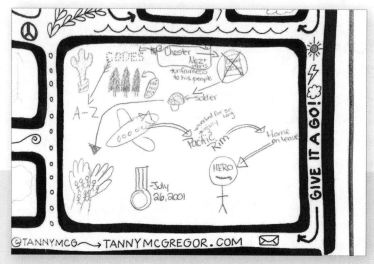

## try this

Sketchnote sequential information with symbols and text in sketchnoted timelines for greater understanding.

Taylor, a high school student, listened to a retelling of the biography of Chester Nez, one of the original Navajo code talkers. Taylor used symbols and arrows to chronicle Nez's life, paralleling the structure of the article.

Ayla structured this sketchnote as a timeline of a story that chronicles the life of a man who experiences racism against Aboriginals in the 1950s. Ayla captured important events and emotions in this timeline made entirely of symbols.

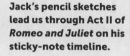

Jack's pencil sketches lead us through Act II of *Romeo and Juliet* on his sticky-note timeline.

# Sketchnoting to Connect with Others

Almost any reason to communicate is a reason to sketchnote! Sketchnotes as messages let us add a personal touch to the message we want to share, giving us fresh ways to layer meaning and emotion as writers. Collaborating with others to sketchnote gives us a visual way to share our thinking and learn from others' thinking.

Cheryl, a principal, used just a few words and pictures, to convey the school's appreciation for their instructional volunteers.

**try this**

Sketchnote a message to an individual or group.

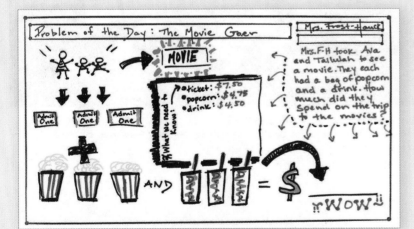

Heather, an elementary math teacher, begins her classes with a sketchnoted "problem of the day." The sketchnote is immediately engaging; it draws students into the scenario; it includes visuals that will help students solve the problem; and it is filled with a sense of excitement (they're going to a movie, after all!) that the word problem doesn't convey.

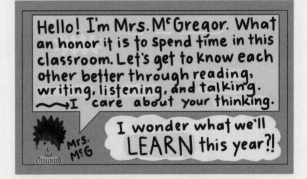

As a literacy coach in multiple schools, I try to let kids know that even though I'm not their classroom teacher, I want to get to know them and I care about their thinking. When I begin working with a class, I project a sketchnoted greeting like this one on the screen. This heartfelt, enthusiastic, and slightly playful introduction helps me begin building relationships with students during the first visits of the year.

129

## try this

Sketchnote with others in an enthusiast group.

Cary's fifth-grade students enjoy sketchnoting so much they created the "Sketchy Lunch Bunch." Kids opt to sketchnote during lunch and recess, eating, talking and sketching the time away.

Susan, a university professor, and Johnny, an instructional coach, sketchnote together during a monthly book club meeting. Books + sketchnotes + friendship = a perfect evening.

*try this*

collaborate with others to create a progressive sketchnote.

Created as part of #PassTheSketchnote 2017, an interactive sketchnote experience conceived by @heckawesome and @mospillman, the sketchnote pictured here traveled not only from pen to pen but from continent to continent! Six different sketchnoters contributed, one at a time, adding personalized sketchnote messages to celebrate World Sketchnote Day, January 11. This sketchnoting team included @bencrothers, @claire_ohl, @hmarrs24, @blaho_blaho, @TTmomTT, and me, @TannyMcG. While all of the pieces of the sketchnote relate to World Sketchnote Day, each piece gives a different perspective.

We've come a long way together in this book, you and I. You're reading this months or years after it was written, but somehow it feels like you were there as I typed each word, as I added each photograph and sketchnote to the manuscript. As this book was created, I pictured you sitting in a classroom with me, or in a little coffeeshop after school. I imagined us sharing stories about our students and trading ideas about how sketchnoting might support our own learning and that of our kids. Oh, I wish it were true! There is no replacement for face-to-face conversation about what we do and why we do it. But until that time, when we meet in a crowded classroom or over a strawberry tea, let this book stand in the gap. May our thinking, and that of our students, be released into the world with paper and pen, with stylus and screen . . . with ink and ideas.

# Sketchnoting as a Pathway to Discovery

**Heidi** | GIFTED INTERVENTION
SPECIALIST, GRADES 3 AND 4

As a learner, I started experimenting with sketching as I read. I found that sketching helped me process what I was thinking and organize ideas as I interacted with text. Sketchnoting helped me take notetaking to a new level through the use of color, creative fonts, lines, and other artistic elements. When I sketch I realize that I am thinking carefully about an idea; the act of creating the sketch combines the kinesthetic with the visual. My own personal learning really sticks.

At first I explored sketching when I read professional texts. After reading a chapter, I would go back and comb through my highlighting so that I could reflect on what I just read. I used a large sketchbook and a generous collection of colored pens. It was amazing how engaged I became. New ideas and insights from the reflection became woven into the concepts and theories in the text. Later I found that the visual notes I had crafted were excellent memory aids. I could remember complete ideas from a key word or image I had sketched.

When I introduced sketchnoting to my students as a tool for processing what they read, some were skeptical because they didn't think they could draw well. The more I emphasized "ideas not art"—my favorite quote from Mike Rohde, author of *The Sketchnote Handbook* (2013)—the more they explored. It wasn't long before they were hooked. As they read a text and talked about it with each other, they kept their pencils in hand. Many found they were intently sketching as they were talking and listening to each other. New discoveries emerged.

Along with my students, I continue to use sketchnoting as a strategy when I read to help me unpack my thinking. When I reflect in this way, I focus on what the author wants me to know, what challenges or changes my thinking, and how what I am reading will help me be a better person. These takeaways are shaping my students into readers who think more deeply and critically as well. It is rare that I read something without a pen in my hand anymore!

Sketching doesn't just enhance our reading behaviors. It helps us become better listeners. When our hands are moving and interacting with what we hear to produce something visual, the result is a tangible product we can come back to and contemplate later. As a result, sketchnoting is a way to increase what we remember. I can look back on a sketch after sitting in a meeting or listening to a speaker, and no matter how engaged (or not) I was, my understanding improves when I sketch. This is a realization my students are starting to make and the excitement is contagious!

**Heidi has learned to sketchnote right alongside her students. Her pathway of discovery has helped her decide where her students might go next.**

# Thinkers & Artists

For as long as I can remember, I have used and loved the ampersand. When I was in elementary school, before I even knew its real name, I swirled my simple version of the ampersand on my papers and could not understand why teachers wouldn't let me use it instead of expanding it into a word.

Along with never having to play dodge ball ever again, an advantage of being grown up is that I can use the ampersand as often as I like. I love the way my pen moves when I make it. Satisfying. To me, the ampersand is such a beautiful character. The curves. The asymmetry. The interesting variations.

The history of the ampersand is as interesting as the shape is unique. For example, did you know that the ampersand was used as early as the first century A.D.? Or that some textbooks in the 1800s listed the ampersand as the twenty-seventh letter of the alphabet? Even now, the ampersand continues its presence into the twenty-first century as an indispensable character in computer programming languages. Perhaps these seem like fun facts that you'll never

need to recall. But the ampersand has another meaningful purpose to me, and it has everything to do with sketchnoting and the reason I wrote this book.

Repeatedly, when referring to sketchnoting, I read and hear the following phrase used, or something close to it: "It's about the thinking, not the art." I've even said it myself a time or two. I understand why people say this: it's a clear way to say that sketchnoting is *not* meaningless decoration or affectation. Some of the most talented and creative sketchnoters I know hold this to be true. But, when I hear it, and even as I've said it, something feels uncomfortable to me. I've learned to recognize and consider this unsettled feeling when it arises, and most always my reflections clarify my beliefs.

I started wondering why this phrase didn't exactly ring true. Don't I believe that thinking is the most important part of visual notetaking? Of course I do. Over time, though, I began to realize that to value something (thinking), I don't have to devalue something else (art). I even wondered, "What if the sketchnoter's thinking is made more memorable, more meaningful, BECAUSE of the art?" What if it is an AND, not an OR? Ampersand to the rescue.

If it weren't for art, the thinking in a sketchnote would look a lot like every other kind of notetaking. If it weren't for art, the thinking in a sketchnote might not be unleashed in a unique, personalized flood of ideas. If it weren't for art, sketchnotes wouldn't be sketchnotes.

If it seems like I'm splitting hairs or that it is only an issue of semantics, consider this. Maybe what's important here is how we define the word *art*. We toss around the word *art* without a thought. We talk about the art of leadership, how an appliance is state of the art, and call someone artsy if they paint or draw well. We imply with all of these that to be artistic is to be part of an elite group, to be able to be or create

in ways that few can achieve. If this is how art is defined, then yes: sketchnoting is about the thinking, not the art. I do not ascribe to that limiting definition any longer, however.

Artmaking is not "a magical gift bestowed only by the gods" explain David Bayles and Ted Orland (1993) in their eye-opening book *Art & Fear* (notice the ampersand!). They invite us to uncover our assumptions about art and reconsider our beliefs. Ponder a few of their illuminating thoughts:

- Art is made by ordinary people.
- The flawless creature wouldn't need to make art.
- Becoming an artist consists of learning to accept yourself.
- Artmaking involves skills that can be learned.
- What matters is the process.
- You learn how to make your work by making your work.

Over time, this is what I've come to believe: Every student I meet, and every teacher, too, can engage in the sketchnoting process as *both* thinker and artist. Art is not reserved for a talented few. Art is not limited to those who can draw well or paint a recognizable picture. Art is made by ordinary people and can help us represent our ideas in extraordinary ways.

Thinkers & artists.

The ampersand makes all

the difference.

# Appendix A

# a Sketchnoter's TREASURE TROVE

books about sketchnoting, art & design, twitter handles & hashtags, apps & more!

# → read ♥♥

books about art, creativity & sketchnoting ←

**ORBITING** *the* **GIANT HAIRBALL** | Mackenzie

**ART & FEAR** | BAYLES & ORLAND

**VISUAL NOTE-TAKING** *for* **EDUCATORS** | PILLARS

**THE DOODLE REVOLUTION** | BROWN

Sketchnotes *for* Educators | Duckworth

**intention** | Burvall & Ryder

SYLLABUS | BARRY

**SKETCHNOTING IN SCHOOL** | PERRY, WEIMAR & BELL

The Sketchnote Handbook | ROHDE

**FOLLOW:**

@woodard_julie

@SketchnoteArmy

@xLontrax

@DoodleRev

@sylviaduckworth

@rohdesign

@wendi322

@mospillman

@sketchbkproject

@heckawesome

@TannyMcG

# explore:
## on TWITTER

# #hashtags

# #ReadSketchThink

# #doodlerevolution

# #edusketch  #sketchnotearmy

# #passthesketchnote

# #sketch50

# #sketchnotes #sketchnoting

# SKETCH

apps & ideas → to TRY!

TAYASUI sketches

@PROCREATE

Procreate

GOOGLE drawings

@FiftyThree

Ed Emberley's

DRAWING BOOK series

Paper by 53

GOOGLE → QUICK DRAW

@explainevrythng

autodesk SKETCH-BOOK

www.thenounproject.com

Appendix B

# Sketchnoting Templates

## *Collect Visual Roadmaps for the Journey Ahead*

Consider this template collection as you explore visual notetaking experiences with your students. The use of a template is optional, yet even experienced sketchnoters sometimes use a template as an instant organizational tool. If a template helps to organize your thinking so that you can concentrate more on the content of your notes instead of the way they are arranged, a template is a welcomed support.

All of the templates are download-able and printable and can be found online on the Heinemann website under the *Ink & Ideas* companion resources tab at Hein.pub/InkAndIdeas.

The template I use in Chapter 2's launching lesson is highly structured for optimal support. It can be used when introducing students to the basic features of sketchnotes, giving them a defined space in which to practice and a larger place to "give it a go." Whenever possible, I reproduce this template on 11" x 17" paper to give it a "placemat" feel.

Download at Hein.pub/InkAndIdeas

Creating a stylized template of your own provides a dedicated structure to use at any time. I keep extra copies of a favorite template in my paper notebook and a digital version in my tablet. Students might choose to create a personalized template of their own to encourage ownership and creativity in their notetaking process.

There are endless ways to prepare the page and allow thinking to freely flow. The following basic templates can be used across grade levels, across content areas, and for all sorts of purposes in and out of school. These templates complement the organizational ideas outlined in Chapter 3. Experiment and enjoy!

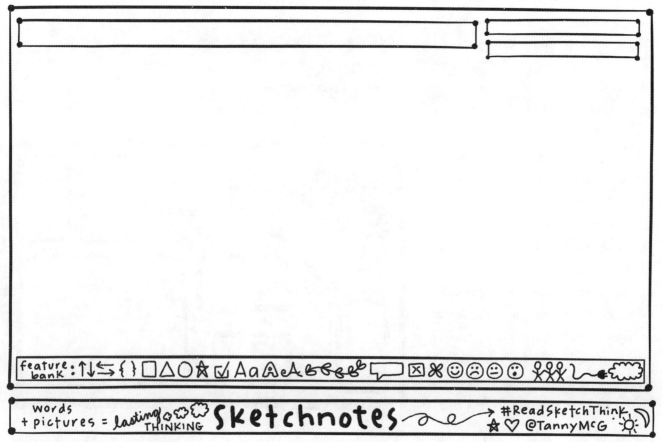

Download at Hein.pub/InkAndIdeas

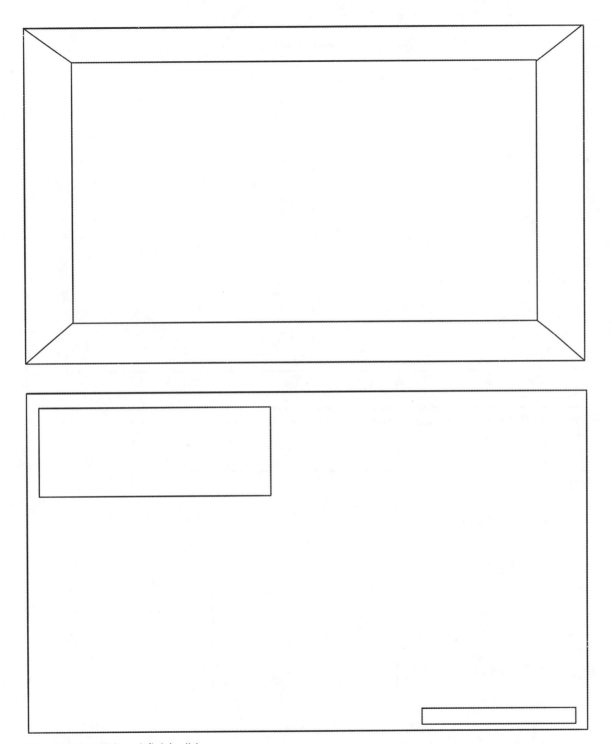

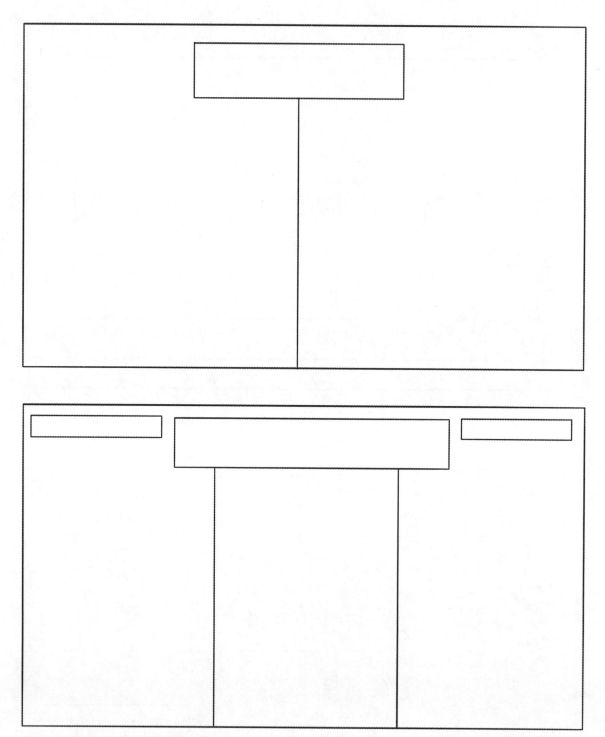

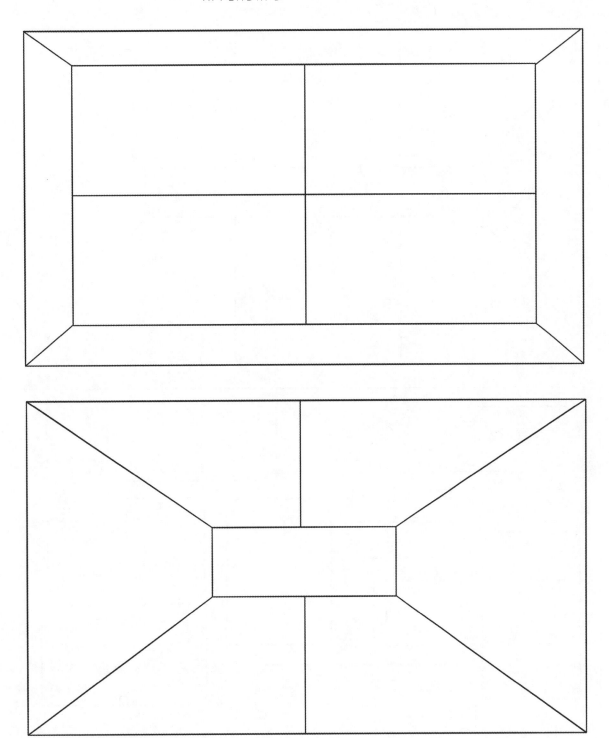

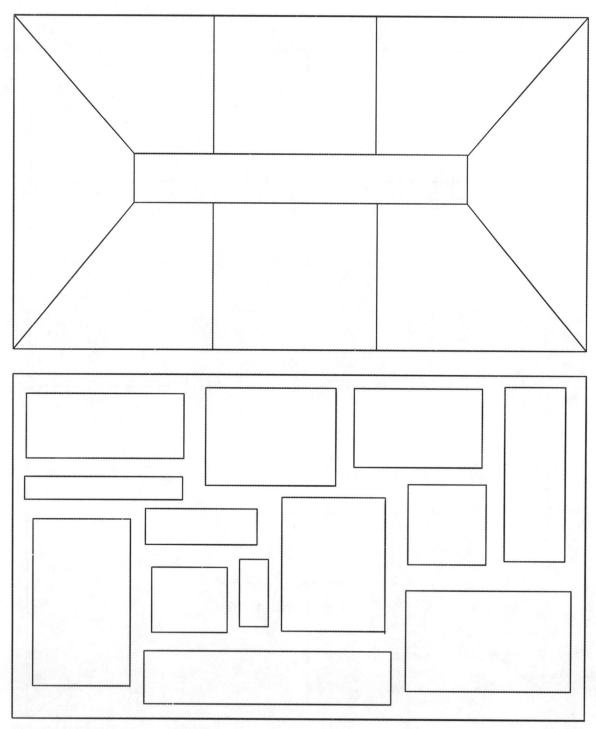

# References

"About This Collection—Alexander Graham Bell Family Papers at the Library of Congress." The Library of Congress. Accessed April 04, 2018. www.loc.gov /collections/alexander-graham-bell-papers/about-this-collection/.

Allard, William Albert. William Albert Allard—Thoughts. Accessed April 04, 2018. www.williamalbertallard.com/thoughts.php.

Andrade, Jackie. 2010. "What Does Doodling Do?" *Applied Cognitive Psychology* 24 (1): 100–106. doi:10.1002/acp.1561.

"The Art and Craft of Storytelling." *The Moth*. Accessed April 04, 2018. www .themoth.org/.

Barry, Lynda. 2015. *Syllabus: Notes from an Accidental Professor.* Montreal: Drawn & Quarterly.

"Basquiat: The Unknown Notebooks." Cleveland Museum of Art. 2017. Accessed April 04, 2018. www.clevelandart.org/exhibitions/basquiat-unknown-notebooks.

Bates, Karl Leif. 2011. "Mining 50 Years of Chimpanzee Data." Accessed April 04, 2018. https://research.duke.edu/stories/fifty-years-chimpanzee-data.

Baum, L. Frank. 1900. *The Wonderful Wizard of Oz.* Chicago: George M. Hill Company.

Bayles, David, and Ted Orland. 1993. *Art & Fear: Observations on the Perils (and Rewards) of Artmaking.* Santa Cruz, CA: Image Continuum Press.

Bergman, Marilyn, and Alan Bergman. 1968. "The Windmills of Your Mind." Song composed by Michel Legrand and Alan Bergman. Performed by Sting, 1999.

Bligh, Donald A. 2000. What's the Use of Lectures? New York: Jossey-Bass.

Blume, Judy. 1972. *Tales of a Fourth Grade Nothing.* New York: Dutton.

Bradstreet, Anne. [ca. 1650]. "To My Dear and Loving Husband." Poets.org. Accessed April 05, 2018. www.poets.org/poetsorg/poem/my-dear-and-loving -husband.

Brown, Brené. 2015. "Big Strong Magic." Episode 12 of *Magic Lessons* podcast hosted by Elizabeth Gilbert. https://soundcloud.com/riverheadbooks/ep-12-big -strong-magic.

———. 2010. "The Power of Vulnerability." Lecture, TEDx, Houston. www.Ted/com /talks/brane_brown_on_vulnerability.

———. 2013. "Why Your Critics Aren't the Ones Who Count." December 4 Lecture, 99u, Alice Tully Hall, New York.

Brown, Sunni. 2015. *Doodle Revolution: Unlock the Power to Think Differently.* New York: Portfolio Penguin.

———. "Doodlers, Unite!" 2011. Lecture, TED2011, California, Long Beach. www.ted.com/talks/suni_brown.

Brubeck, Dave. "Blue Rondo à la Turk." Time Out, recorded June–August 1959. Columbia Records.

Burvall, Amy, and Dan Ryder. 2017. *Intention: Critical Creativity in the Classroom.* Irvine, CA: EdTechTeam Press.

Christensen, Tanner. Creative Something. Accessed April 4, 2018. https:// creativesomething.net/.

Cincinnati Art Museum website. Accessed April 4, 2018. www.cincinnatiartmuseum. org/.

Curry, John Steuart. *The Tornado.* 1932. The Metropolitan Museum of Art, New York. Accessed April 4, 2018. www.metmuseum.org/art/collection /search/373353.

De La Rosa, Gabriella. "Between Naturalism and Fantasy: The Art of Beatrix Potter." National Trust. Accessed April 4, 2018. www.nationaltrust.org.uk/features/ between-naturalism-and-fantasy-the-art-of-beatrix-potter.

DeZure, Deborah, Matthew Kaplan, and Martha A. Deerman. 2001. *Research on Student Notetaking: Implications for Faculty and Graduate Student Instructors.* Occasional Paper No. 16. Ann Arbor: Center for Research on Learning and Teaching.

Dickinson, Emily. "The Brain Is Wider than the Sky." Accessed April 5, 2018. www .bartleby.com/113/1126.html.

Duckworth, Sylvia. 2016. *Sketchnotes for Educators.* Irvine: Edtechteam Press.

"Einstein Archives Online." Einstein Archives Online. Accessed April 4, 2018. www.alberteinstein.info/.

Emberley, Ed. 2006. *Ed Emberley's Drawing Book: Make a World.* New York: LB Kids.

FiftyThree Inc. 2018. "Paper by FiftyThree." Apple App Store, Vers. 4.0.11. https:// itunes.apple.com/us/app/paper-by-fiftythree/id506003812?mt=8 (accessed 5 April 2018).

Fleischman, Paul. 1997. *Seedfolks.* NewYork: HarperCollins.

Frazee, Marla. 2006. *Walk On!: A Guide for Babies of All Ages.* Orlando: Harcourt.

Fries-Gaither, Jessica. 2017. *Notable Notebooks: Scientists and Their Writings*. Arlington, VA: National Science Teachers.

Goodman, Timothy. 2015. *Sharpie Art Workshop Techniques & Ideas for Transforming Your World*. Beverly, MA: Rockport Publishers.

Graham, Chrissie. "The Contact Lens." *The Moth*. Accessed May 10, 2016. https://themoth.org/stories/the-contact-lens.

Greenberg, David. 2007. *Presidential Doodles: Two Centuries of Scribbles, Scratches, Squiggles & Scrawls from the Oval Office*. New York: Basic Books.

Harvey, Stephanie, and Anne Goudvis. 2007. *Strategies That Work: Teaching Comprehension for Understanding and Engagement,* 2nd Edition. Portland, ME: Stenhouse Publishers.

Hattie, John. 2009. *Visible Learning: A Synthesis of over 800 Meta-Analyses Relating to Achievement*. London: Routledge.

Hinton, S. E. 1967. *The Outsiders*. New York: Viking.

Hoyt, Linda. 2009. *Revisit, Reflect, Retell: Time-Tested Strategies for Teaching Reading Comprehension*. Portsmouth, NH: Heinemann.

"Interrogating Texts: Six Reading Habits to Develop in Your First Year at Harvard." Harvard Library Research Guides. Accessed April 4, 2018. https://guides.library.harvard.edu/sixreadinghabits.

"Inventions, Games, & Contraptions." Mark Twain's Notebook—Inventions, Games, and Contraptions, Mark Twain at Play, University of California, Berkeley. Accessed April 4, 2018. http://bancroft.berkeley.edu/Exhibits/mtatplay/inventions/notebook.html.

"Jim Knight's One Best Question." 2017. *Box of Crayons*. https://boxofcrayons.com/2018/02/jim-knights-one-best-question/.

Johnstone, A. H, and W. Y. Su. 1994. "Lectures—a Learning Experience?" *Education in Chemistry*, 31, (1): 75–76, 79.

Kahlo, Frida, Carlos Fuentes, and Sarah M. Lowe. 2005. *The Diary of Frida Kahlo: An Intimate Self-Portrait*. New York: Harry N. Abrams.

Kaimal, Girija, Kendra Ray, and Juan Muniz. 2016. "Reduction of Cortisol Levels and Participants' Responses Following Art Making." *Art Therapy* 33, (2): 74–80. doi:10.1080/07421656.2016.1166832.

Kidd, Dustin. 2002. "Book Review: *What's the Use of Lectures?*" Center for Teaching Excellence, Spring. http://cte.virginia.edu/resources/book-review-whats-the-use-of-lectures/.

Kiewra, Kenneth A., Nelson F. Dubois, David Christian, Anne McShane, Michelle Meyerhoffer, and David Roskelly. 1991. "Note-taking Functions and Techniques." *Journal of Educational Psychology* 83, (2): 240–245. doi:10.1037/0022-0663.83.2.240.

Kleon, Austin. "Blog." Austin Kleon. Accessed April 4, 2018. www.austinkleon.com/.

——. *Steal Like an Artist: 10 Things Nobody Told You About Being Creative*. 2012. New York: Workman Publishers.

"Leonardo Da Vinci's Notebook." 2015. The British Library. Accessed April 4, 2018. www.bl.uk/collection-items/leonardo-da-vinci-notebook.

"Literacy Worldwide—The International Literacy Association." International Literacy Association. Accessed April 4, 2018. www.literacyworldwide.org/.

Lowry, Lois. 1989. *Number the Stars*. Boston: Houghton Mifflin Harcourt.

Mackenzie, Gordon. 1998. *Orbiting the Giant Hairball: A Corporate Fool's Guide to Surviving with Grace*. New York: Penguin Group.

"Mary Anning." Lyme Regis Museum. Accessed April 4, 2018. www.lymeregismuseum.co.uk/collection/mary-anning/.

Marzano, Robert. 2010. "The Art and Science of Teaching: Representing Knowledge Nonlinguistically." *Educational Leadership* 67, (8): 84–86.

Marzano, Robert J., and Mark W. Haystead. 2009. *Meta-Analytic Synthesis of Studies Conducted at Marzano Research Laboratory on Educational Strategies*. Report. Centennial: Marzano Research.

McCandless, David. "Information Is Beautiful." Information Is Beautiful. Accessed April 4, 2018. www.informationisbeautiful.net/.

McDonnell, Patrick. 2016. *The Little Gift of Nothing*. New York: LB Kids.

McGregor, Tanny. 2007. *Comprehension Connections: Bridges to Strategic Reading*. Portsmouth, NH: Heinemann.

Montgomery, L. M. 1908. *Anne of Green Gables*. New York: Grosset & Dunlap.

Mothersbaugh, Mark. 2014. *Mark Mothersbaugh—Myopia*. New York: Princeton Architectural Press.

Mueller, Pam A., and Daniel M. Oppenheimer. 2014. "The Pen Is Mightier Than the Keyboard." *Psychological Science* 25, (6): 1159–1168 doi:10.1177/0956797614524581.

"The Notebook of William Blake." 2014. The British Library. Accessed April 4, 2018. www.bl.uk/collection-items/the-notebook-of-william-blake.

Ogle, Donna M. 1986. "K-W-L: A Teaching Model That Develops Active Reading of Expository Text." *The Reading Teacher* 39, (6): 564–570. doi:10.1598/rt.39.6.11.

"Ohio Writing Project." Ohio Writing Project—Miami University. Accessed April 4, 2018. http://miamioh.edu/cas/academics/departments/english/academics/ohio-writing-project/.

"Pablo Picasso—Artist Biography." Pablo Picasso Paintings, Prints & Biography. Accessed April 4, 2018. www.pablopicasso.net/.

Paivio, Allan. 1971. *Imagery and Verbal Processes*. New York: Holt, Rinehart and Winston.

——. 1990. *Mental Representations: A Dual Coding Approach*. New York: Oxford University Press.

Palacio, R. J. 2012. *Wonder*. New York: Alfred A. Knopf.

Parton, Dolly. 2016. *Coat of Many Colors*. New York: Grosset & Dunlap, an Imprint of Penguin Random House.

Pearson, P. David, L. Roehler, J. A. Dole, and G. G. Duffy. 1992. "Developing Expertise in Reading Comprehension." In *What Research Has to Say About Reading Instruction*, edited by S. Jay Samuels and Alan Farstrup. 2nd ed. Newark, DE: International Reading Association.

Perkins, David. 2003. "Making Thinking Visible." Harvard Graduate School of Education/Project Zero. Visible Thinking. http://www.visiblethinkingpz.org/VisibleThinking_html_files/06_AdditionalResources/MakingThinkingVisible_DP.pdf.

Perry, Karin, Holly Weimar, and Mary Ann Bell. 2018. *Sketchnoting in School: Discover the Benefits (and Fun) of Visual Note Taking*. Lanham, MD: Rowman & Littlefield.

Pett, Mark, and Gary Rubinstein. 2011. *The Girl Who Never Made Mistakes*. Naperville, IL: Sourcebooks Jabberwocky.

Pillars, Wendi. 2016. *Visual Note-Taking for Educators: A Teacher's Guide to Student Creativity*. New York: Norton.

Pipes, Taylor. "Taking Note: How Note-Taking Improves Reading—An Interview with Shane Parrish." *Evernote Blog*. May 31, 2016. Accessed April 4, 2018. https://blog.evernote.com/blog/2016/05/06/taking-note-how-note-taking-improves-reading-an-interview-with-shane-parrish/.

Pippin's Story. National Gallery of Art. Accessed April 4, 2018. www.nga.gov/education/teacher/lessons-activities/counting-art/pippin.html.

Popova, Maria. 2015. "A Simple Exercise to Increase Well-Being and Lower Depression from Martin Seligman, Founding Father of Positive Psychology." *Brain Pickings*. www.brainpickings.org/2014/02/18/martin-seligman-gratitude-visit-three-blessings/.

Purdy, Charles. 2015. "Make It Anywhere: Timothy Goodman." Make It Anywhere: Timothy Goodman | Create. https://create.adobe.com/2015/3/23/make_it_anywhere_timothy_goodman.html.

"Purpose & Beliefs." Target Corporate. Accessed April 6, 2018. https://corporate.target.com/about/purpose-beliefs.

"Resources." The Jim Henson Legacy—Resources. Accessed April 4, 2018. www.jimhensonlegacy.org/facts-and-things/resources.

Reynolds, Peter H. 2004. *Ish*. Cambridge, MA: Candlewick Press.

——. *The Dot.* 2008. London: Walker.

——. *Sky Color.* 2014. Toronto: CNIB.

Riddles, Libby. 2002. *Storm Run: The Story of the First Woman to Win the Iditarod Sled Dog Race.* Seattle, WA: Sasquatch Books.

Roam, Dan. 2013. *The Back of the Napkin: Solving Problems and Selling Ideas with Pictures.* New York: Portfolio.

——. *Draw to Win: A Crash Course on How to Lead, Sell, and Innovate with Your Visual Mind.* 2016. New York: Portfolio/Penguin.

Robinson, Sharon. 2017. *The Hero Two Doors Down: Based on the True Story of Friendship Between a Boy and a Baseball Legend.* New York: Scholastic.

Rohde, Mike. 2013. *The Sketchnote Handbook: The Illustrated Guide to Visual Note Taking.* San Francisco, CA: Peachpit Press.

——. *The Sketchnote Workbook: Advanced Techniques for Taking Visual Notes You Can Use Anywhere.* 2015. San Francisco, CA: Peachpit Press.

Saltzberg, Barney. 2010. *Beautiful Oops!* New York: Workman Publishers.

"See Inside the Da Vinci Notebook That Cost Bill Gates $30 Million." 2015. *National Geographic.* Accessed April 04, 2018. www.nationalgeographic.com.au/history /see-inside-the-da-vinci-notebook-that-cost-bill-gates-30-million.aspx.

Shakespeare, William. 2016. *Romeo and Juliet.* Edited by Peter Holland. Penguin Classics.

Shovan, Laura. 2016. *Last Fifth Grade of Emerson Elementary.* New York: Wendy Lamb Books, an imprint of Random House Children's Books.

Shurtliff, Liesl. 2017. *Red: The True Story of Red Riding Hood.* New York: Scholastic.

Staykov, Hristo. 2018. Amaziograph, Vers. 4.01. Apple App Store. https://itunes .apple.com/us/app/amaziograph/id586076398?mt=8.

Stead, Tony, and Linda Hoyt. 2012. *Explorations in Nonfiction Writing.* Portsmouth, NH: Heinemann.

Sweet, Melissa. Melissa Sweet. Accessed April 4, 2018. http://melissasweet.net/.

Tarshis, Lauren. 2015. *I Survived the Great Chicago Fire, 1871.* New York: Scholastic.

"Thomas A. Edison Papers." The Thomas A. Edison Papers at Rutgers University. Accessed April 4, 2018. http://edison.rutgers.edu/.

Thomas, Nigel J. T. 2014. "Dual Coding and Common Coding Theories of Memory." *Stanford Encyclopedia of Philosophy.* https://plato.stanford.edu/entries /mental-imagery/theories-memory.html.

Thoreau, Henry David. 2012. *Walden, Or, Life in the Woods; and "Civil Disobedi-ence."* Edited by W. S. Merwin and William Howarth. New York: Signet Classics.

Ulin, David L. 2018. *Lost Art of Reading: Why Books Matter in a Distracted Time*. Seattle: Sasquatch Books.

VanDerwater, Amy Ludwig. *Sharing Our Notebooks* [blog]. Accessed April 4, 2018. www.sharingournotebooks.amylv.com/.

Verne, Jules. "Biography." IMDb. Accessed April 6, 2018. www.imdb.com/name /nm0894523/bio.

"Virginia Woolf's Travel and Literary Notebook, 1906–1909." British Library Collection Items. Accessed April 4, 2018. https://www.bl.uk/collection-items /virginia-woolfs-travel-and-literary-notebook-1906-09.

Visible Thinking. Accessed April 4, 2018. www.Visiblethinkingpz.org/.

Voiklis, Charlotte Jones. 2018. "Madeleine L'Engle, Author of *A Wrinkle in Time*— The Official Website." Madeleine L'Engle.  https://www.madeleinelengle.com/.

Wammes, Jeffrey D., Melissa E. Meade, and Myra A. Fernandes. 2016. "The Drawing Effect: Evidence for Reliable and Robust Memory Benefits in Free Recall." *Quarterly Journal of Experimental Psychology* 69, (9): 1752–1776. doi:10.1080/17470218.201 5.1094494.

Whitman, Walt. "Sometimes with One I Love." Poetry Foundation. Accessed April 6, 2018. https://www.poetryfoundation.org/poems/50322/sometimes-with-one-i-love.

———. "When I Heard the Learn'd Astronomer." Poetry Foundation. Accessed April 5, 2018. www.poetryfoundation.org/poems/45479/when-i-heard-the-learnd -astronomer.

*Words and Pictures*. 2013. Directed by Fred Schepisi. Performed by Clive Owen and Juliette Binoche. Latitude Productions.

Zeldman, Jeffrey. 2008. Twitter post. https://twitter.com/zeldman /statuses/804159148.

Zemelman, Steven, Harvey Daniels, and Arthur A. Hyde. 2012. *Best Practice: Bringing Standards to Life in America's Classrooms*. Portsmouth, NH: Heinemann.

Zimmer, Eric. 2016. "135: Michelle Segar." *The One You Feed*. Podcast. www.oneyoufeed.net/michelle-segar/.